Psalms

With
Introductions
by Martin Luther

**Introductions translated
by Bruce A. Cameron**

PUBLISHING HOUSE

Copyright © 1993 Concordia Publishing House
3558 S. Jefferson Avenue, St. Louis, MO 63118-3968
Manufactured in the United States of America

Library of Congress Cataloging-in-Publication Data

Bible. O.T. Psalms. English. New International. 1993.
     Psalms / with introductions by Martin Luther ; introductions translated by Bruce A. Cameron.
     ISBN 0-570-04623-8
     1. Bible. O.T. Psalms—Criticism, interpretation, etc. I. Cameron, Bruce A. II. Luther, Martin, 1483–1546. Summarien ueber die Psalmen. English. 1993. III. Title.
     BS1422   1993b
     223'.205208—dc20   93-31311

1 2 3 4 5 6 7 8 9 10   02 01 00 99 98 97 96 95 94 93

PREFACE

Martin Luther loved the Psalter. It was his daily prayer book as a monk, the topic of his initial lectures as a professor. The first book he ever offered for publication was a translation and explanation of the seven penitential psalms. By the time he completed his translation of the Bible into German, he had published six separate editions of the Psalter. His lectures and commentaries on the psalms fill five full volumes in the American Edition of Luther's Works.

In all his writings, however, Luther only once prepared a work that commented on all 150 psalms. *The Summaries of the Psalms, 1531*—here presented for the first time in English—were published in 1532 and 1533 as a companion for his final comprehensive revision of the Psalter (1531). In these short introductions, Luther allows us a glimpse into his theology and his prayer life. He shows that he understood the Psalter as a Christ-centered book and how he prayed each psalm as a Christian prayer.

Luther demonstrates his approach to the psalms in two ways: First, he classifies each psalm as a psalm of prophecy, instruction, comfort, prayer, or thanks—or some combination of the above. For Luther, the psalms carried this content beyond the original writer and original setting. They are words of prophecy, instruction, prayer, comfort, and thanks for us today.

Second, he assigns each psalm to one of the Ten Commandments and to one of the petitions of the Lord's Prayer. He says that the psalms "belong to," "flow from," or even "are in" these petitions and commandments. In actual practice, he related nearly all the psalms to the first three commandments—having one God, honoring his name, hearing his Word—and to the first three petitions—concerning God's name, his kingdom, and his will. All the other commandments and petitions merely fill out what these first words express. Luther discontinued this second classification scheme after Psalm 31. In a long comment at that point, he says that the reader has seen enough examples to understand the insight that the psalmist and every Christian can find in the Tables of Moses and the Our Father.

Luther's approach to the psalms is notable, particularly because it is Christ centered. For him, all aspects of Christian life, including the psalms, relate to Christ. Even the psalmists' down-to-earth requests for protection and thanks for deliverance Luther applied to his own circumstances and life as a Christian. The psalmists asked for blessing and gave thanks for blessings as members of the covenant people of God, relying on God's grace, trusting his promises, worshiping in his temple, receiving his forgiveness. Yet all of these—covenant, grace, promise, temple, and forgiveness—found their fulfillment in Jesus Christ. Christ "is himself the God whom we are exhorted to worship." When the psalmist exults that God's "love endures forever," Luther responds that *Christ* "stands hidden" in that phrase.

The Old Testament psalms not only permit us to see Christ in them, they require it. Resurrection, eternity, a universal kingdom, forgiveness, even grace and blessing—each ultimately has its home and its fulfillment in Jesus Christ. To be faithful to the witness of the New Testament and to the witness of the psalms themselves is to find Christ throughout the Psalter. He fulfills its promises and comfort with his life; he invites to himself the prayers and worship the psalms speak about. Finally, the psalms that require holiness and righteousness to be prayed aright are prayers that no one can offer unless covered by grace and forgiveness, but grace and forgiveness are ultimately gifts of Jesus Christ.

This book uses the New International Version of the psalms. The translation of Luther's *Summaries* is based on the Weimar Edition, vol. 38, and the St. Louis Edition, vol. 4. For this devotional edition, we have omitted some of Luther's references to the specific adversaries of his day and supplemented some of his shorter summaries with comments from his other writings.

At the conclusion of his summaries, Luther requested:

> If anyone is pleased with my poor assistance by these summaries, I ask that he not insert them into the Psalter between the psalms.

We are overruling this request, as Concordia Publishing House did a century ago (when it printed the *Altenberger Bibelwerk*), confident that Luther's advice on reading the psalms can help contemporary Christians find their way to some of the riches of the Psalter. Luther, however, was firm about what was important:

> I prefer to see the text stand alone by itself, unmixed with anything else. Some of these summaries are really a brief commentary, and it would not be proper if, placed in the middle of the text, these summaries would loom larger than the psalms themselves. With this, may God bless you. Amen.

Bruce A. Cameron
St. Louis
February 18, 1993

LUTHER'S SUMMARIES
AND THE PSALMS

LUTHER'S INTRODUCTION

The entire Psalter may be treated in a fivefold fashion, that is, we may divide it into five groups.

First, some psalms *prophesy*. They speak, for example, of Christ and the church or what will happen to the saints. This class includes all the psalms that contain promises and warnings—promises for the godly and warnings for the ungodly.

Second, there are psalms of *instruction*, which teach us what we should do and what we should avoid, in accordance with the law of God. This class includes all the psalms that condemn human doctrines and praise the Word of God.

Third, there are psalms of *comfort*, which strengthen and comfort the saints in their troubles and sorrows but rebuke and terrify the tyrants. This class includes all the psalms that comfort, exhort, stimulate endurance, or rebuke the tyrants.

Fourth are the psalms of *prayer*, in which we call on God, praying in all kinds of distress. To this class belong all the psalms that lament or mourn or cry out against our foes.

Fifth, are the psalms of *thanks*, in which God is praised and glorified for all his blessings and help. This class includes all the psalms that praise God for his works. These are the psalms of the first rank, and for their sake the Psalter was created; therefore it is called in Hebrew *Sefer Tehillim*, that is, a praise book or book of thanksgiving.

Now, we should understand that the psalms, with all their verses, cannot always be classified so precisely and exactly into these groups. At times one psalm might contain two, three, or even all five classifications, so that one psalm may belong in all five divisions, with prophecy, instruction, comfort, prayer, and thanksgiving lying next to one another. However, this is the intention, that the reader may understand that the Psalter deals with these five topics. The classifications are a help, so that we might more easily understand the Psalter, become adapted to it, and also be able to learn and keep it.

PSALM 1

Psalm 1 is a psalm of comfort. It admonishes us to gladly hear and learn God's Word and brings us the comfort that, in so doing, we will have many and great benefits. Just as a palm tree by the water grows green and brings fruit despite all heat and cold and the like, so also all our words and works will prosper despite all enemies. Human doctrines do not have this benefit, but, as the wind blows the chaff away, so they also pass away. For God says that he is pleased by those who study his Word, but the others he allows to perish.

This psalm flows from the third commandment; indeed, it is part of that commandment, for the command to honor the Sabbath is itself the command to hear and learn God's Word. It is also included in the second and third petitions of the Our Father, for in these we pray for God's kingdom and his will, both of which are conveyed by his Word.

PSALM 1

Blessed is the man who does not walk in the counsel of the wicked or stand in the way of sinners or sit in the seat of mockers. But his delight is in the law of the Lord, and on his law he meditates day and night. He is like a tree planted by streams of water, which yields its fruit in season and whose leaf does not wither. Whatever he does prospers.

Not so the wicked! They are like chaff that the wind blows away. Therefore the wicked will not stand in the judgment, nor sinners in the assembly of the righteous.

For the Lord watches over the way of the righteous, but the way of the wicked will perish.

PSALM 2

Psalm 2 is a prophecy of Christ, that he would suffer and through his suffering become King and Lord of the whole world. Within this psalm stands a warning against the world's kings and lords: if, instead of honoring and serving this king, they seek to persecute and blot him out, they shall perish. This psalm also contains the promise that those who believe in him will be blessed.

This psalm flows from the first commandment, in which God promises to be our God, who will help us in every trouble and will work all good for us—just as he has, through Christ, delivered us from sin, death, and hell and brought us to eternal life. This blessing is what we pray for in the second petition of the Our Father: that his kingdom come.

PSALM 2

Why do the nations conspire and the peoples plot in vain? The kings of the earth take their stand and the rulers gather together against the Lord and against his Anointed One. "Let us break their chains," they say, "and throw off their fetters."

The One enthroned in heaven laughs; the Lord scoffs at them. Then he rebukes them in his anger and terrifies them in his wrath, saying, "I have installed my King on Zion, my holy hill."

I will proclaim the decree of the Lord: He said to me, "You are my Son; today I have become your Father. Ask of me, and I will make the nations your inheritance, the ends of the earth your possession. You will rule them with an iron scepter; you will dash them to pieces like pottery."

Therefore, you kings, be wise; be warned, you rulers of the earth. Serve the Lord with fear and rejoice with trembling. Kiss the Son, lest he be angry and you be destroyed in your way, for his wrath can flare up in a moment. Blessed are all who take refuge in him.

PSALM 3

Psalm 3 is a psalm of prayer in which we follow the example of David. He prayed this prayer in his distress when he was expelled by his son Absalom, and his prayer was granted to him. At the end, David glorifies God for being a true helper and keeper for all of his people who call on him in distress.

This psalm belongs to the first commandment, that God will be our God and our help. The psalm is in the seventh petition of the Our Father, in which we pray to be delivered from all evil.

PSALM 3

A psalm of David. When he fled from his son Absalom.

O Lord, how many are my foes! How many rise up against me! Many are saying of me, "God will not deliver him."

But you are a shield around me, O Lord; you bestow glory on me and lift up my head. To the Lord I cry aloud, and he answers me from his holy hill.

I lie down and sleep; I wake again, because the Lord sustains me. I will not fear the tens of thousands drawn up against me on every side.

Arise, O Lord! Deliver me, O my God! Strike all my enemies on the jaw; break the teeth of the wicked.

From the Lord comes deliverance. May your blessing be on your people.

PSALM 4

Psalm 4 is a psalm of comfort, which is at the same time a psalm of prayer and instruction. It teaches us to trust in God when things go wrong and rebukes the ungodly, who concern themselves over vain gods and fleshly comfort and yet will not bear to wait confidently for God, who is the highest comfort. God surprises us by how he deals with his saints. At first, he abandons them and tries their faith and patience. The ungodly, on the other hand, want to have a full and secure belly. If anyone talks to them about faith and patience, they mock and despise him and say, "Can this fool tell us what is good? Yes, you be patient until a roast chicken flies into your mouth. Trust in that and you will starve!"

This psalm belongs to the first commandment. It teaches and urges us to hope in God and endure hardship and every need with patience, and it rebukes the faithless and impatient. The psalm is included in the third and seventh petitions, in which we pray that God's will be done and that we be delivered from evil. It can also be in the fourth petition, when we ask for our daily bread, that is, for peace and all the necessities of life in the face of every earthly need.

PSALM 4

For the director of music. With stringed instruments. A psalm of David.

Answer me when I call to you, O my righteous God. Give me relief from my distress; be merciful to me and hear my prayer.

How long, O men, will you turn my glory into shame? How long will you love delusions and seek false gods?

Know that the Lord has set apart the godly for himself; the Lord will hear when I call to him.

In your anger do not sin; when you are on your beds, search your hearts and be silent. Offer right sacrifices and trust in the Lord.

Many are asking, "Who can show us any good?" Let the light of your face shine upon us, O Lord. You have filled my heart with greater joy than when their grain and new wine abound. I will lie down and sleep in peace, for you alone, O Lord, make me dwell in safety.

PSALM 5

Psalm 5 is a psalm of prayer against the false teachers and the rebellious spirits. It harshly condemns both their glistening teaching and their works, by which—under the name of God—they do great harm to the pure Word of God and the true worship of God. The psalm prays for the righteous, that is, for the pure Word of God and the pure worship of God. In the last verse it promises that such a prayer will be heard and the rebellious spirits will be condemned.

This psalm belongs to the second and third commandments, in which we are commanded to keep both God's name and God's Word holy. It belongs to the first and second petitions of the Our Father, in which we pray that God's name, honor, and kingdom will be advanced.

PSALM 5

For the director of music. For flutes. A psalm of David.

Give ear to my words, O Lord, consider my sighing. Listen to my cry for help, my King and my God, for to you I pray. In the morning, O Lord, you hear my voice; in the morning I lay my requests before you and wait in expectation.

You are not a God who takes pleasure in evil; with you the wicked cannot dwell. The arrogant cannot stand in your presence; you hate all who do wrong. You destroy those who tell lies; bloodthirsty and deceitful men the Lord abhors.

But I, by your great mercy, will come into your house; in reverence will I bow down toward your holy temple. Lead me, O Lord, in your righteousness because of my enemies—make straight your way before me.

Not a word from their mouth can be trusted; their heart is filled with destruction. Their throat is an open grave; with their tongue they speak deceit. Declare them guilty, O God! Let their intrigues be their downfall. Banish them for their many sins, for they have rebelled against you.

But let all who take refuge in you be glad; let them ever sing for joy. Spread your protection over them, that those who love your name may rejoice in you. For surely, O Lord, you bless the righteous; you surround them with your favor as with a shield.

PSALM 6

Psalm 6 is a psalm of prayer. It laments the great yet hidden suffering of the conscience when, on account of sins, one's faith and hope are tormented by the law and anger of God and driven to despair or erring faith. This suffering is called elsewhere in the Psalter "the bonds of death" and "the ropes of hell," or "the misery of death" and "the anguish of hell." At the end the psalmist sees that his prayer has been heard. He is therefore a trustworthy example for those who find themselves in such affliction, so that they may not remain in it. He rebukes the workers of evil, that is, the false saints who generally hate and persecute such afflicted people. Because their comfort is in their own holiness, they know nothing of these trials. They are therefore utter enemies of the true faith.

This psalm belongs to the first and second commandments because it commends the struggle of those who believe in God and pray against sin and death. It is in the first petition of the Our Father, as are all other psalms of prayer, because its prayer is that God's name be called upon and blessed.

PSALM 6

For the director of music. With stringed instruments. According to sheminith. *A psalm of David.*

O Lord, do not rebuke me in your anger or discipline me in your wrath. Be merciful to me, Lord, for I am faint; O Lord, heal me, for my bones are in agony. My soul is in anguish. How long, O Lord, how long?

Turn, O Lord, and deliver me; save me because of your unfailing love. No one remembers you when he is dead. Who praises you from the grave?

I am worn out from groaning; all night long I flood my bed with weeping and drench my couch with tears. My eyes grow weak with sorrow; they fail because of all my foes.

Away from me, all you who do evil, for the Lord has heard my weeping. The Lord has heard my cry for mercy; the Lord accepts my prayer. All my enemies will be ashamed and dismayed; they will turn back in sudden disgrace.

PSALM 7

Psalm 7 is also a psalm of prayer. It laments over slanderers who accuse the saints and their teachings of being riotous, opposed to the authorities, and disturbing the peace. In this way Shimei the Benjaminite (2 Sam. 16:5–14) slandered the pious David as if David had stolen King Saul's kingdom. In the same way, Christ was also accused before Pilate, and even now slanderers defame the Gospel. David fights against this affliction with prayer and cries to God of his innocence. By his own example, he shows us that such a prayer was granted, so that we might have comfort. The psalm also threatens the slanderers and oppressors and holds before them the example of those who perish before they accomplished the evil they intended. It belongs, like the preceding psalm, in the second commandment and the first petition.

PSALM 7

A shiggaion *of David, which he sang to the Lord concerning Cush, a Benjamite.*

O Lord my God, I take refuge in you; save and deliver me from all who pursue me, or they will tear me like a lion and rip me to pieces with no one to rescue me.

O Lord my God, if I have done this and there is guilt on my hands— if I have done evil to him who is at peace with me or without cause have robbed my foe—then let my enemy pursue and overtake me; let him trample my life to the ground and make me sleep in the dust.

14

Arise, O Lord, in your anger; rise up against the rage of my enemies. Awake, my God; decree justice. Let the assembled peoples gather around you. Rule over them from on high; let the Lord judge the peoples. Judge me, O Lord, according to my righteousness, according to my integrity, O Most High. O righteous God, who searches minds and hearts, bring to an end the violence of the wicked and make the righteous secure.

My shield is God Most High, who saves the upright in heart. God is a righteous judge, a God who expresses his wrath every day. If he does not relent, he will sharpen his sword; he will bend and string his bow. He has prepared his deadly weapons; he makes ready his flaming arrows.

He who is pregnant with evil and conceives trouble gives birth to disillusionment. He who digs a hole and scoops it out falls into the pit he has made. The trouble he causes recoils on him; his violence comes down on his own head.

I will give thanks to the Lord because of his righteousness and will sing praise to the name of the Lord Most High.

PSALM 8

Psalm 8 is a prophecy of Christ—his sufferings, resurrection, and kingly rule over all creatures. This kingdom shall be established by the voice of children, that is, it will be established not by sword or armor but by Word and faith alone. This psalm belongs in the first commandment, that God intends to be our God, and the second petition, as was stated in Psalm 2 above.

PSALM 8

For the director of music. According to gittith. *A psalm of David.*

O Lord, our Lord, how majestic is your name in all the earth!

You have set your glory above the heavens. From the lips of children and infants you have ordained praise because of your enemies, to silence the foe and the avenger.

When I consider your heavens, the work of your fingers, the moon and the stars, which you have set in place, what is man that you are mindful of him, the son of man that you care for him? You made him a little lower than the heavenly beings and crowned him with glory and honor.

You made him ruler over the works of your hands; you put everything under his feet: all flocks and herds, and the beasts of the field, the birds of the air, and the fish of the sea, all that swim the paths of the seas.

O Lord, our Lord, how majestic is your name in all the earth!

PSALM 9

Psalm 9 is also a prophecy of the people of Christ, the holy Christian church. They suffer, following the example of Christ, and their blood is continually being shed. The psalm however gives this prophecy thankfully and comfortingly, so that it might well be called a psalm of thanks and comfort. The Christian (and especially the holy martyrs) here thank God and are comforted by the fact that God never leaves them. No, the more they are persecuted, the more he multiplies them, as some of the persecutors convert and become Christians and the others perish. This psalm belongs in the first commandment and in the second petition, as was stated in the preceding psalm.

Psalm 9

For the director of music. To the tune of "The Death of the Son." A psalm of David.

I will praise you, O Lord, with all my heart; I will tell of all your wonders. I will be glad and rejoice in you; I will sing praise to your name, O Most High.

My enemies turn back; they stumble and perish before you. For you have upheld my right and my cause; you have sat on your throne, judging righteously. You have rebuked the nations and destroyed the wicked; you have blotted out their name for ever and ever. Endless ruin has overtaken the enemy, you have uprooted their cities; even the memory of them has perished.

The Lord reigns forever; he has established his throne for judgment, He will judge the world in righteousness; he will govern the peoples with justice. The Lord is a refuge for the oppressed, a stronghold in times of trouble. Those who know your name will trust in you, for you, Lord, have never forsaken those who seek you.

Sing praises to the Lord, enthroned in Zion; proclaim among the nations what he has done. For he who avenges blood remembers; he does not ignore the cry of the afflicted.

O Lord, see how my enemies persecute me! Have mercy and lift me up from the gates of death, that I may declare your praises in the gates of the Daughter of Zion and there rejoice in your salvation. The nations have fallen into the pit they have dug; their feet are caught in the net they have hidden. The Lord is known by his justice; the wicked are ensnared by the work of their hands.

The wicked return to the grave, all the nations that forget God. But the needy will not always be forgotten, nor the hope of the afflicted ever perish. Arise, O Lord, let not man triumph; let the nations be judged in your presence. Strike them with terror, O Lord; let the nations know they are but men.

PSALM 10

Psalm 10 is a psalm of prayer. It laments over the enemies of the kingdom of Christ who terrify Christendom with force and cunning. They direct the sword of worldly tyranny over the body and the net of false teaching over the soul. But as it says in verse 7 (''his mouth is full of cursing, lies, and deception''), they can do no more than curse, that is, excommunicate and condemn; lie, that is bring about false doctrine and false worship; and deceive, that is, delude and make a fool of the world concerning its goods, honor, power, body, and soul. But in the end, the psalm shows our comfort, that such abomination shall perish with the end of the world. The psalm belongs in the second commandment and in the first petition, as all psalms of prayer.

PSALM 10

Why, O Lord, do you stand far off? Why do you hide yourself in times of trouble?

In his arrogance the wicked man hunts down the weak, who are caught in the schemes he devises. He boasts of the cravings of his heart; he blesses the greedy and reviles the Lord. In his pride the wicked does not seek him; in all his thoughts there is no room for God. His ways are always prosperous; he is haughty and your laws are far from him; he sneers at all his enemies. He says to himself, "Nothing will shake me; I'll always be happy and never have trouble." His mouth is full of curses and lies and threats; trouble and evil are under his tongue. He lies in wait near the villages; from ambush he murders the innocent, watching in secret for his victims. He lies in wait like a lion in cover; he lies in wait to catch the helpless; he catches the helpless and drags them off in his net. His victims are crushed, they collapse; they fall under his strength. He says to himself, "God has forgotten; he covers his face and never sees."

Arise, Lord! Lift up your hand, O God. Do not forget the helpless.

Why does the wicked man revile God? Why does he say to himself, "He won't call me to account"? But you, O God, do see trouble and grief; you consider it to take it in hand. The victim commits himself to you; you are the helper of the fatherless. Break the arm of the wicked and evil man; call him to account for his wickedness that would not be found out.

The Lord is king for ever and ever; the nations will perish from his land. You hear, O Lord, the desire of the afflicted; you encourage them, and you listen to their cry, defending the fatherless and the oppressed, in order that man, who is of the earth, may terrify no more.

PSALM 11

The 11th psalm is a psalm of prayer. It laments over the heretics and false interpreters of the Scriptures who lead the people away from the true ground of faith and bring them to their mountains, that is, their great high holiness of works. To that end, they mock the true teacher and say, ''What shall the righteous do?'' But the psalm ends with this comfort, that God will certainly see this. The false teachers will be condemned and the righteous will remain. This prayer can thus be an example for us. This psalm belongs in the second commandment and the first petition, as all psalms of prayer.

PSALM 11

For the director of music. Of David.

In the Lord I take refuge. How then can you say to me: ''Flee like a bird to your mountain. For look, the wicked bend their bows; they set their arrows against the strings to shoot from the shadows at the upright in heart. When the foundations are being destroyed, what can the righteous do?''

The Lord is in his holy temple; the Lord is on his heavenly throne. He observes the sons of men; his eyes examine them. The Lord examines the righteous, but the wicked and those who love violence his soul hates. On the wicked he will rain fiery coals and burning sulfur; a scorching wind will be their lot.

For the Lord is righteous, he loves justice; upright men will see his face.

PSALM 12

The 12th psalm is a psalm of prayer. It laments over the teachers who are always inventing new little discoveries and filling up God's kingdom everywhere with these new services to God. For where human doctrines once go in, there is no stop or end to them, but they increase more and more. They load down the poor conscience beyond all limit and work so that few true saints may remain. Against all this, the psalm comforts us that God will awaken his salvation, that is, his Word, which confidently storms against this work of straw. He will free the imprisoned conscience. This does not happen however without cross and agony. As silver is purified in the fire, so they also must suffer in the meantime, and by this means become ever more pure and perceive the truth so much more clearly. This psalm belongs in the second and third commandments and the first and second petitions.

Psalm 12

For the director of music. According to sheminith. *A psalm of David.*

Help, Lord, for the godly are no more; the faithful have vanished from among men. Everyone lies to his neighbor; their flattering lips speak with deception.

May the Lord cut off all flattering lips and every boastful tongue that says, "We will triumph with our tongues; we own our lips—who is our master?"

"Because of the oppression of the weak and the groaning of the needy, I will now arise," says the Lord. "I will protect them from those who malign them." And the words of the Lord are flawless, like silver refined in a furnace of clay, purified seven times.

O Lord, you will keep us safe and protect us from such people forever. The wicked freely strut about when what is vile is honored among men.

PSALM 13

The 13th psalm is a psalm of prayer against the sorrow or sadness of the spirit that comes at times from the devil himself, at times from those who act against us with spite and evil tricks. As a result, we are cast down and grieve when we see such evil aligned against us. But prayer is stronger than all misfortune. This psalm gives us here an example by which we certainly may be comforted and learn in every kind of calamity not to become anxious or downcast, nor let these troubles eat at our hearts. Instead we learn to turn to prayer, crying to God about all of these things. We know that we will be heard and finally be delivered, as James 5:13 also says: "If anyone is troubled let him pray." This psalm belongs in the second commandment and the first and last petitions, that we may be delivered from evil.

PSALM 13

For the director of music. A psalm of David.

How long, O Lord? Will you forget me forever? How long will you hid your face from me? How long must I wrestle with my thoughts and every day have sorrow in my heart? How long will my enemy triumph over me?

Look on me and answer, O Lord my God. Give light to my eyes, or I will sleep in death; my enmey will say, "I have overcome him," and my foes will rejoice when I fall.

But I trust in your unfailing love; my heart rejoices in your salvation. I will sing to the Lord, for he has been good to me.

PSALM 14

The 14th psalm is a prophecy and a psalm of instruction which teaches us that all human doctrine and life without faith is nothing but an abomination before God. Such worship of God is only belly worship by which the ungodly fatten themselves, devouring the goods of the people. They do not know or understand anything of the true worship of God, although they teach and praise the law of God. Moreover, they profane and blaspheme God's Word whenever it rebukes them at all. They will listen to nothing about trust or faith in God.

These people must be resisted by prayer. This prayer shall be heard, as the last verse says, and the Gospel of Christ shall come. Thus this psalm reproves especially those who tormented the people with the law. When it speaks of the help for Zion, it is promising or prophesying of the coming of Christ, for the Gospel and the Spirit have come from Zion.

This psalm belongs to the first and the third commandments because it praises God's Word, promises Christ, and also reproves the hypocrites and devouring teachers or belly-teachers. It is in the first and second petitions, in which we pray for his name and his kingdom.

PSALM 14

For the director of music. Of David.

The fool says in his heart, ''There is no God.'' They are corrupt, their deeds are vile; there is no one who does good.

The Lord looks down from heaven on the sons of men to see if there are any who understand, any who seek God. All have turned aside, they have together become corrupt; there is no one who does good, not even one.

Will evildoers never learn—those who devour my people as men eat bread and who do not call on the Lord? There they are, overwhelmed with dread, for God is present in the company of the righteous. You evildoers frustrate the plans of the poor, but the Lord is their refuge.

Oh, that salvation for Israel would come out of Zion! When the Lord restores the fortunes of his people, let Jacob rejoice and Israel be glad!

PSALM 15

The 15th psalm is a psalm of instruction which teaches the true understanding of the law, the truly good life, and true good works. These are all fruits of the Spirit and of faith: to live blameless before God through true faith, to do right to the neighbor, and to turn away from the evil ways and from the hypocrisy of the ungodly, by which they serve God with fraudulent works and omit the true works. This psalm belongs to the third commandment, concerning the Sabbath, in which we are to hear and learn God's Word, and it is in the third petition.

PSALM 15

A psalm of David.

Lord, who may dwell in your sanctuary? Who may live on your holy hill?

He whose walk is blameless and who does what is righteous, who speaks the truth from his heart and has no slander on his tongue, who does his neighbor no wrong and casts no slur on his fellow man, who despises a vile man but honors those who fear the Lord, who keeps his oath even when it hurts, who lends his money without usury and does not accept a bribe against the innocent.

He who does these things will never be shaken.

PSALM 16

The 16th psalm is a prophecy of the suffering and resurrection of Christ, as the apostles themselves powerfully indicate (Acts 2:25 and 13:35). It clearly gives witness that Christ has discarded as idolatry the old law with its sacrifices and worship and has chosen other saints and another people to be his heirs. It belongs to the first, second, and third commandments, for it announces the new praise, work, Word, and worship that would come into the world in Christ, after the old worship. It is in the first and second petitions.

PSALM 16

A miktam *of David.*

Keep me safe, O God, for in you I take refuge.

I said to the Lord, "You are my Lord; apart from you I have no good thing."

As for the saints who are in the land, they are the glorious ones in whom is all my delight. The sorrows of those will increase who run after other gods. I will not pour out their libations of blood or take up their names on my lips.

Lord, you have assigned me my portion and my cup; you have made my lot secure. The boundary lines have fallen for me in pleasant places; surely I have a delightful inheritance.

I will praise the Lord, who counsels me; even at night my heart instructs me. I have set the Lord always before me. Because he is at my right hand, I will not be shaken.

Therefore my heart is glad and my tongue rejoices; my body also will rest secure, because you will not abandon me to the grave, nor will you let your Holy One see decay. You have made known to me the path of life; you will fill me with joy in your presence, with eternal pleasures at your right hand.

PSALM 17

The 17th psalm is a psalm of prayer. It laments over the false teachers and the ''scrupulous'' saints who, by human doctrines and works, lead people away from God's Word. They persecute the true doctrine and hate the cross of Christ. With their doctrines and works, they seek only that they might have good things, praise, and freedom here on earth, and that they might not have to suffer want. It belongs to the second and third commandments and in the first petition, that God's Word and name may be sanctified.

PSALM 17

A prayer of David.

Hear, O Lord, my righteous plea; listen to my cry. Give ear to my prayer—it does not rise from deceitful lips. May my vindication come from you; may your eyes see what is right.

Though you probe my heart and examine me at night, though you test me, you will find nothing; I have resolved that my mouth will not sin. As for the deeds of men—by the word of your lips I have kept myself from the ways of the violent. My steps have held to your paths; my feet have not slipped.

I call on you, O God, for you will answer me; give ear to me and hear my prayer. Show the wonder of your great love, you who save by your right hand those who take refuge in you from their foes. Keep me as the apple of your eye; hide me in the shadow of your wings from the wicked who assail me, from my mortal enemies who surround me.

They close up their callous hearts, and their mouths speak with arrogance. They have tracked me down, they now surround me, with eyes alert, to throw me to the ground. They are like a lion hungry for prey, like a great lion crouching in cover.

Rise up, O Lord, confront them, bring them down; rescue me from the wicked by your sword. O Lord, by your hand save me from such men, from men of this world whose reward is in this life.

You still the hunger of those you cherish; their sons have plenty, and they store up wealth for their children. And I—in righteousness I will see your face; when I awake, I will be satisfied with seeing your likeness.

PSALM 18

The 18th psalm is a psalm of thanks in which, as the title declares, David thanks God that he has delivered him from all his enemies, such as Saul, the heathen, Absalom, and the rebellious Israelites. He relates that he was in deadly distresses and that God has helped him out of them. In the manner of a prophet he shows how God helped him as God had helped Israel in Egypt. He praises God, who held back his enemies, and thanks God for his help against the disobedient and the rebels, such as Seba and most of Israel were (2 Samuel 20). He had so many enemies and hostile subjects, that even the heathen foreigners (he says here) were more obedient than his own people.

Consequently, everyone needs to keep this psalm as an example of how we should thank God for his help when God delivers us out of our troubles. Whoever wants to explain this psalm spiritually may think of David as a Christian, standing against the heathen, the tyrants, the heretics, and the false Christians. From all of these, Christ and all his people will finally be delivered. It belongs in the second commandment and in the first petition, because it thanks God and praises his holy name.

PSALM 18

For the director of music. Of David the servant of the Lord. He sang to the Lord the words of this song when the Lord delivered him from the hand of all his enemies and from the hand of Saul. He said:

I love you, O Lord, my strength.

The Lord is my rock, my fortress and my deliverer; my God is my rock, in whom I take refuge. He is my shield and the horn of my salvation, my stronghold. I call to the Lord, who is worthy of praise, and I am saved from my enemies.

The cords of death entangled me; the torrents of destruction overwhelmed me. The cords of the grave coiled around me; the snares of death confronted me. In my distress I called to the Lord; I cried to my God for help. From his temple he heard my voice; my cry came before him, into his ears.

The earth trembled and quaked, and the foundations of the mountains shook; they trembled because he was angry. Smoke rose from his nostrils; consuming fire came from his mouth, burning coals blazed out of it. He parted the heavens and came down; dark clouds were under his feet. He mounted the cherubim and flew; he soared on the wings of the wind. He made darkness his covering, his canopy around him—the dark rain clouds of the sky. Out of the brightness of his presence clouds advanced, with hailstones and bolts of lightning. The Lord thundered from heaven; the voice of the Most High resounded. He shot his arrows and scattered the enemies, great bolts of lightning and routed them. The valleys of the sea were exposed and the foundations of the earth laid bare at your rebuke, O Lord, at the blast of breath from your nostrils.

He reached down from on high and took hold of me; he drew me out of deep waters. He rescued me from my powerful enemy, from my foes, who were too strong for me. They confronted me in the day of my disaster, but the Lord was my support. He brought me out into a spacious place; he rescued me because he delighted in me.

The Lord has dealt with me according to my righteousness; according to the cleanness of my hands he has rewarded me. For I have kept the ways of the Lord; I have not done evil by turning from my God. All his laws are before me; I have not turned away from his decrees. I have been blameless before him and have kept myself from sin. The Lord has rewarded me according to my righteousness, according to the cleanness of my hands in his sight.

To the faithful you show yourself faithful, to the blameless you show yourself blameless, to the pure you show yourself pure, but to the crooked you show yourself shrewd. You save the humble but bring low those whose eyes are haughty. You, O Lord, keep my lamp burning; my God turns my darkness into light. With your help I can advance against a troop; with my God I can scale a wall.

As for God, his way is perfect; the word of the Lord is flawless. He is a shield for all who take refuge in him. For who is God besides the Lord? And who is the Rock except our God? It is God who arms me with strength and makes my way perfect. He makes my feet like the feet of a deer; he enables me to stand on the heights. He trains my hands for battle; my arms can bend a bow of bronze. You give me your shield of victory, and your right hand sustains me; you stoop down to make me great. You broaden the path beneath me, so that my ankles do not turn.

I pursued my enemies and overtook them; I did not turn back till they were destroyed. I crushed them so that they could not rise; they fell beneath my feet. You armed me with strength for battle; you made my adversaries bow at my feet. You made my enemies turn their backs in flight, and I destroyed my foes. They cried for help, but there was no one to save them—to the Lord, but he did not answer. I beat them as fine as dust borne on the wind; I poured them out like mud in the streets.

You have delivered me from the attacks of the people; you have made me the head of nations; people I did not know are subject to me. As soon as they hear me, they obey me; foreigners cringe before me. They all lose heart; they come trembling from their strongholds.

The Lord lives! Praise be to my Rock! Exalted be God my Savior! He is the God who avenges me, who subdues nations under me, who saves me from my enemies. You exalted me above my foes; from violent men you rescued me. Therefore I will praise you among the nations, O Lord; I will sing praises to your name. He gives his king great victories; he shows unfailing kindness to his anointed, to David and his descendants forever.

PSALM 19

The 19th psalm is a prophecy. It speaks of how the Gospel would spread to all the world, as far as the heavens extend. Day and night it would be spread, not only in Hebrew but in all languages. Just as the sun (which he uses for an example) shines and gives warmth everywhere, so also will the new law of the Gospel enlighten and teach all kinds of people, comforting and purifying them. In this way the old law is removed, which was not so pure, bright, lovely, or imperishable. This psalm belongs in the third commandment, for it proclaims the true Sabbath in which God's Word is taught and believed.

PSALM 19

For the director of music. A psalm of David.

The heavens declare the glory of God; the skies proclaim the work of his hands. Day after day they pour forth speech; night after night they display knowledge. There is no speech or language where their voice is not heard. Their voice goes out into all the earth, their words to the ends of the world.

In the heavens he has pitched a tent for the sun, which is like a bridegroom coming forth from his pavilion, like a champion rejoicing to run his course. It rises at one end of the heavens and makes its circuit to the other; nothing is hidden from its heat.

The law of the Lord is perfect, reviving the soul. The statutes of the Lord are trustworthy, making wise the simple. The precepts of the Lord are right, giving joy to the heart. The commands of the Lord are radiant, giving light to the eyes. The fear of the Lord is pure, enduring forever. The ordinances of the Lord are sure and altogether righteous. They are more precious than gold, than much pure gold; they are sweeter than honey, than honey from the comb. By them is your servant warned; in keeping them there is great reward.

Who can discern his errors? Forgive my hidden faults. Keep your servant also from willful sins; may they not rule over me. Then will I be blameless, innocent of great transgression.

May the words of my mouth and the meditation of my heart be pleasing in your sight, O Lord, my Rock and my Redeemer.

PSALM 20

The 20th psalm is a psalm of prayer. It prays specifically for emperor, kings, princes, governors, and all those who sit in any seat of authority. The psalm prays that God would grant them grace to rule peacefully and well, giving them good fortune and victory over their enemies. For wherever good earthly order is established by the reason and power of governor and princes, people do not earnestly and heartily pray for them. So that people might pray for them, the psalm declares that only the greatest fool, totally blind, would presume to rule land and people out of his own head. This psalm belongs in the second commandment, as do all the psalms of prayer, in which one calls on God's name. It is in the third petition, that God's will and not the devil's might be done.

PSALM 20

For the director of music. A psalm of David.

May the Lord answer you when you are in distress; may the name of the God of Jacob protect you. May he send you help from the sanctuary and grant you support from Zion. May he remember all your sacrifices and accept your burnt offerings.

May he give you the desire of your heart and make all your plans succeed. We will shout for joy when you are victorious and will lift up our banners in the name of our God. May the Lord grant all your requests.

Now I know that the Lord saves his anointed; he answers him from his holy heaven with the saving power of his right hand. Some trust in chariots and some in horses, but we trust in the name of the Lord our God. They are brought to their knees and fall, but we rise up and stand firm.

O Lord, save the king! Answer us when we call!

PSALM 21

The 21st psalm is a prophecy of the kingdom of Christ, the kingdom which is and remains eternally and spiritually before God. At the same time, it also announces that those who reject this kingdom shall be destroyed. This psalm belongs in the first commandment and the second petition, for it announces a new worship and kingdom.

PSALM 21

For the director of music. A psalm of David.

O Lord, the king rejoices in your strength. How great is his joy in the victories you give! You have granted him the desire of his heart and have not withheld the request of his lips. You welcomed him with rich blessings and placed a crown of pure gold on his head.

He asked you for life, and you gave it to him—length of days, for ever and ever. Through the victories you gave, his glory is great; you have bestowed on him splendor and majesty. Surely you have granted him eternal blessings and made him glad with the joy of your presence. For the king trusts in the Lord; through the unfailing love of the Most High he will not be shaken.

Your hand will lay hold on all your enemies; your right hand will seize your foes. At the time of your appearing you will make them like a fiery furnace. In his wrath the Lord will swallow them up, and his fire will consume them. You will destroy their descendants from the earth, their posterity from mankind. Though they plot evil against you and devise wicked schemes, they cannot succeed; for you will make them turn their backs when you aim at them with drawn bow.

Be exalted, O Lord, in your strength; we will sing and praise your might.

PSALM 22

The 22nd psalm is a prophecy of the suffering and resurrection of Christ and of the Gospel, which the entire world shall hear and receive. Beyond all other texts, it clearly shows Christ's torment on the cross, that he was pierced hand and foot and his limbs stretched out so that his bones could have been counted. Nowhere in the other prophets can one find so clear a description. It is indeed one of the chief psalms. It belongs in the first commandment, for it promises a new worship of God. It is in the first and second petitions.

PSALM 22

For the director of music. To the tune of "The Doe of the Morning." A psalm of David.

My God, my God, why have you forsaken me? Why are you so far from saving me, so far from the words of my groaning? O my God, I cry out by day, but you do not answer, by night, and am not silent.

Yet you are enthroned as the Holy One; you are the praise of Israel. In you our fathers put their trust; they trusted and you delivered them. They cried to you and were saved; in you they trusted and were not disappointed.

But I am a worm and not a man, scorned by men and despised by the people. All who see me mock me; they hurl insults, shaking their heads: "He trusts in the Lord; let the Lord rescue him. Let him deliver him, since he delights in him."

Yet you brought me out of the womb; you made me trust in you even at my mother's breast. From birth I was cast upon you; from my mother's womb you have been my God. Do not be far from me, for trouble is near and there is no one to help.

Many bulls surround me; strong bulls of Bashan encircle me. Roaring lions tearing their prey open their mouths wide against me. I am poured out like water, and all my bones are out of joint. My heart has turned to wax; it has melted away within me. My strength is dried up like a potsherd, and my tongue sticks to the roof of my mouth; you lay me in the dust of death. Dogs have surrounded me; a band of evil men has encircled me, they have pierced my hands and my feet. I can count all my bones; people stare and gloat over me. They divide my garments among them and cast lots for my clothing.

But you, O Lord, be not far off; O my Strength, come quickly to help me. Deliver my life from the sword, my precious life from the power of the dogs. Rescue me from the mouth of the lions; save me from the horns of the wild oxen.

I will declare your name to my brothers; in the congregation I will praise you. You who fear the Lord, praise him! All you descendants of Jacob, honor him! Revere him, all you descendants of Israel! For he has not despised or disdained the suffering of the afflicted one; he has not hidden his face from him but has listened to his cry for help.

From you comes the theme of my praise in the great assembly; before those who fear you will I fulfill my vows. The poor will eat and be satisfied; they who seek the Lord will praise him—may your hearts live forever! All the ends of the earth will remember and turn to the Lord, and all the families of the nations will bow down before him, for dominion belongs to the Lord and he rules over the nations.

All the rich of the earth will feast and worship; all who go down to the dust will kneel before him—those who cannot keep themselves alive. Posterity will serve him; future generations will be told about the Lord. They will proclaim his righteousness to a people yet unborn—for he has done it.

PSALM 23

The 23rd psalm is a psalm of thanks in which a Christian heart praises and thanks God for teaching him and keeping him on the right way, comforting and protecting him in every danger through his holy Word. He compares himself to a sheep which a faithful shepherd leads into fresh grass and cool water. In addition, he shows the table, the cup, and oil also as images from the Old Testament worship and calls it all God's Word, as it is also called rod and staff, grass, water, and the way of righteousness. This psalm belongs in the third commandment and in the second petition.

PSALM 23

A psalm of David.

The Lord is my shepherd, I shall not be in want. He makes me lie down in green pastures, he leads me beside quiet waters, he restores my soul. He guides me in paths of righteousness for his name's sake. Even though I walk through the valley of the shadow of death, I will fear no evil, for you are with me; your rod and your staff, they comfort me.

You prepare a table before me in the presence of my enemies. You anoint my head with oil; my cup overflows. Surely goodness and love will follow me all the days of my life, and I will dwell in the house of the Lord forever.

PSALM 24

The 24th psalm is a prophecy of the coming worldwide kingdom of Christ. It calls on the ''doors'' of the world, that is, the kings and princes, to make way for the kingdom of Christ. They and those who for the most part rage against him (Psalm 2) say, ''Who is this king of glory?'' as if they were to say, ''This beggar! Yes, this heretic! This criminal! Shall he be a king and shall we yield and submit to him? We shall not!'' In this way the psalm shows that God's Word will certainly be condemned and persecuted. This psalm belongs in the first commandment and in both the third commandment and the third petition.

PSALM 24

Of David. A psalm.

The earth is the Lord's, and everything in it, the world, and all who live in it; for he founded it upon the seas and established it upon the waters. Who may ascend the hill of the Lord? Who may stand in his holy place? He who has clean hands and a pure heart, who does not lift up his soul to an idol or swear by what is false. He will receive blessing from the Lord and vindication from God his Savior. Such is the generation of those who seek him, who seek your face, O God of Jacob.

Lift up your hearts, O you gates; be lifted up, you ancient doors, that the King of glory may come in. Who is this King of glory? The Lord strong and mighty, the Lord mighty in battle. Lift up your heads, O you gates; lift them up, you ancient doors, that the King of glory may come in. Who is he, this King of glory? The Lord Almighty—he is the King of glory.

PSALM 25

The 25th psalm is a psalm of prayer in which the righteous pray that God will make them godly, forgive their sins, guard them from sin and shame, and finally deliver them from all enemies and all evil. Along with this it mocks the false, self-centered spirits and teachers. It belongs to the second commandment and the second petition.

PSALM 25

Of David.

To you, O Lord, I lift up my soul; in you I trust, O my God. Do not let me be put to shame, nor let my enemies triumph over me. No one whose hope is in you will ever be put to shame, but they will be put to shame who are treacherous without excuse.

Show me your ways, O Lord, teach me your paths; guide me in your truth and teach me, for you are God my Savior, and my hope is in you all day long. Remember, O Lord, your great mercy and love, for they are from of old. Remember not the sins of my youth and my rebellious ways; according to your love remember me, for you are good, O Lord.

Good and upright is the Lord; therefore he instructs sinners in his ways. He guides the humble in what is right and teaches them his way. All the ways of the Lord are loving and faithful for those who keep the demands of his covenant. For the sake of your name, O Lord, forgive my iniquity, though it is great. Who, then, is the man that fears the Lord? He will instruct him in the way chosen for him. He will spend his days in prosperity, and his descendants will inherit the land. The Lord confides in those who fear him; he makes his covenant known to them. My eyes are ever on the Lord, for only he will release my feet from the snare.

Turn to me and be gracious to me, for I am lonely and afflicted. The troubles of my heart have multiplied; free me from my anguish. Look upon my affliction and my distress and take away all my sins. See how my enemies have increased and how fiercely they hate me! Guard my life and rescue me; let me not be put to shame, for I take refuge in you. May integrity and uprightness protect me, because my hope is in you.

Redeem Israel, O God, from all their troubles!

PSALM 26

The 26th psalm is a psalm of prayer which laments the false saints who want to be godly through the works of the law and who condemn the saints who are godly only through God's goodness and grace. It accuses the false saints of willingly accepting bribes. For such saints are certainly pure servants of greed, whose God is their stomach, as St. Paul says (Phil. 3:19). But with all their spiritual hypocrisy and their worldly glory, they are destructive saints. Therefore, it is good to pray that they may not deceive us. This psalm belongs in the third commandment and in the first and second petitions, for it speaks of the worship of God and of his kingdom.

PSALM 26

Of David.

Vindicate me, O Lord, for I have led a blameless life; I have trusted in the Lord without wavering. Test me, O Lord, and try me, examine my heart and my mind; for your love is ever before me, and I walk continually in your truth. I do not sit with deceitful men, nor do I consort with hypocrites; I abhor the assembly of evildoers and refuse to sit with the wicked. I wash my hands in innocence, and go about your altar, O Lord, proclaiming aloud your praise and telling of all your wonderful deeds. I love the house where you live, O Lord, the place where your glory dwells.

Do not take away my soul along with sinners, my life with bloodthirsty men, in whose hands are wicked schemes, whose right hands are full of bribes. But I lead a blameless life; redeem me and be merciful to me.

My feet stand on level ground; in the great assembly I will praise the Lord.

PSALM 27

The 27th psalm is a psalm of thanks. It also, however, prays much and gives us comfort against the false teachers, who give a false witness, blaspheming without any hesitation. For only entirely fool-hardy saints would give a witness, bold and impudent, before God—from whom they have no command! Yet we see it daily; the more foolish and unlearned the people are, the more bold and audacious they are to preach and to teach the whole world. No one knows anything; they alone know all. They prepare themselves to make war and revolt against the true saints and God-fearers. This psalm belongs in the second and first commandments and in the first and second petitions.

PSALM 27

Of David.

The Lord is my light and my salvation—whom shall I fear? The Lord is the stronghold of my life—of whom shall I be afraid? When evil men advance against me to devour my flesh, when my enemies and my foes attack me, they will stumble and fall. Though an army besiege me, my heart will not fear; though war break out against me, even then will I be confident.

One thing I ask of the Lord, this is what I seek: that I may dwell in the house of the Lord all the days of my life, to gaze upon the beauty of the Lord and to seek him in his temple. For in the day of trouble he will keep me safe in his dwelling; he will hide me in the shelter of his tabernacle and set me high upon a rock. Then my head will be exalted above the enemies who surround me; at his tabernacle will I sacrifice with shouts of joy; I will sing and make music to the Lord.

Hear my voice when I call, O Lord; be merciful to me and answer me. My heart says of you, "Seek his face!" Your face, Lord, I will seek. Do not hide your face from me, do not turn your servant away in anger; you have been my helper. Do not reject me or forsake me, O God my Savior. Though my father and mother forsake me, the Lord will receive me. Teach me your way, O Lord; lead me in a straight path because of my oppressors. Do not turn me over to the desire of my foes, for false witnesses rise up against me, breathing out violence.

I am still confident of this: I will see the goodness of the Lord in the land of the living. Wait for the Lord; be strong and take heart and wait for the Lord.

PSALM 28

The 28th psalm is a psalm of prayer which David prayed against Saul and similar enemies. He prayed especially against this evil, that they spoke well to him and acted friendly at times, and yet attempted to kill him—as afterward Absalom also attempted. Joab acted the same against Amasa and Abner, so that David was concerned lest God hold him accountable for this, and therefore he prayed that he might not be carried off with the godless. We can pray this psalm against the tyrants and against the rebellious spirits. For the tyrants portray themselves as friendly, and yet in daily machinations they seek ways to kill and destroy. The rebellious spirits praise God's glory, Word, and worship in highest measure; they want to help all the world and are extraordinarily humble; yet, for all of that, they seek the corruption of souls and are, under sheep's clothing, ravening wolves. This psalm belongs in the third and second commandments and the first and second petitions.

PSALM 28

Of David.

To you I call, O Lord my Rock; do not turn a deaf ear to me. For if you remain silent, I will be like those who have gone down to the pit. Hear my cry for mercy as I call to you for help, as I lift up my hands toward your Most Holy Place.

Do not drag me away with the wicked, with those who do evil, who speak cordially with their neighbors but harbor malice in their hearts. Repay them for their deeds and for their evil work; repay them for what their hands have done and bring back upon them what they deserve. Since they show no regard for the works of the Lord and what his hands have done, he will tear them down and never build them up again.

Praise be to the Lord, for he has heard my cry for mercy. The Lord is my strength and my shield; my heart trusts in him, and I am helped. My heart leaps for joy and I will give thanks to him in song.

The Lord is the strength of his people, a fortress of salvation for his anointed one. Save your people and bless your inheritance; be their shepherd and carry them forever.

PSALM 29

The 29th psalm is a prophecy of the Gospel, that it shall resound with power in all the world and overthrow the wisdom and renown of all kings, princes, lords, and peoples, and Christ alone shall be the only king. He shall be served and glorified with true wisdom and holiness. Therefore he established the flood, Baptism, in which the old Adam is drowned and the new man arises. He gives the name of deserts, forests, and deer to the lands of the earth that were under Jew or Gentile and that have been opened and converted to the Gospel. This psalm belongs in the third commandment and in the second petition.

PSALM 29

A psalm of David.

Ascribe to the Lord, O mighty ones, ascribe to the Lord glory and strength. Ascribe to the Lord the glory due his name; worship the Lord in the splendor of his holiness.

The voice of the Lord is over the waters; the God of glory thunders, the Lord thunders over the mighty waters. The voice of the Lord is powerful; the voice of the Lord is majestic. The voice of the Lord breaks the cedars; the Lord breaks in pieces the cedars of Lebanon. He makes Lebanon skip like a calf, Sirion like a young wild ox. The voice of the Lord strikes with flashes of lightning. The voice of the Lord shakes the desert; the Lord shakes the Desert of Kadesh. The voice of the Lord twists the oaks and strips the forests bare. And in his temple all cry, "Glory!"

The Lord sits enthroned over the flood; the Lord is enthroned as King forever. The Lord gives strength to his people; the Lord blesses his people with peace.

PSALM 30

The 30th psalm is a psalm of thanks in which the psalmist gives thanks that God has redeemed him from the high spiritual afflictions of the devil, which are sadness, depression, terror, despair, doubt, the perils of death, and similar poisonous, fiery darts of the devil. Nevertheless, at the same time he has the comfort that God is only angry for the blink of an eye and does not desire nor will our death or distress but desires rather to see us live and be joyful. This psalm belongs in the second commandment and in the first petition.

PSALM 30

A psalm: A song. For the dedication of the temple. Of David.

I will exalt you, O Lord, for you lifted me out of the depths and did not let my enemies gloat over me. O Lord my God, I called to you for help and you healed me. O Lord, you brought me up from the grave; you spared me from going down into the pit.

Sing to the Lord, you saints of his; praise his holy name. For his anger lasts only a moment, but his favor lasts a lifetime; weeping may remain for a night, but rejoicing comes in the morning.

When I felt secure, I said, "I will never be shaken." O Lord, when you favored me, you made my mountain stand firm; but when you hid your face, I was dismayed.

To you, O Lord, I called; to the Lord I cried for mercy: "What gain is there in my destruction, in my going down into the pit? Will the dust praise you? Will it proclaim your faithfulness? Hear, O Lord, and be merciful to me; O Lord, be my help."

You turned my wailing into dancing; you removed my sackcloth and clothed me with joy, that my heart may sing to you and not be silent. O Lord my God, I will give you thanks forever.

PSALM 31

The 31st psalm is a universal psalm of thanks, a psalm of prayer, and a psalm of comfort, all at the same time. It is spoken in the person of Christ and of his saints, who, on account of the Word of God, are plagued their whole life long—inwardly with fears and troubles; outwardly with persecutions, slander, and contempt. And yet they are comforted and delivered by God out of all of them. This psalm belongs in the second and third commandments and in the first and second petitions.

At this point we will stop pointing out in which commandment and which petition each individual psalm belongs. In the preceding, we have examples enough from which it may be easily determined where each of the following psalms belong. Psalms of prayer belong in the second commandment and the first petition, for they praise God's name and call on him. Psalms of instruction, psalms of comfort, and psalms of thanks all belong in the third commandment as well as the second and in the first and second petitions. For they hallow the true Sabbath with true works and with true worship. And many psalms often belong in all three commandments and petitions.

We have pointed these out so that we might learn well to use and understand the commands of God and the Our Father. We see that the beloved saints and prophets spoke of and devoted themselves so abundantly and in such diverse ways to the first three commandments and petitions. They always treated them anew and afresh, yet without having something new to teach, nor did they go beyond the tables of Moses and the Our Father.

From this we may understand that all the Scriptures and the holy lives of the prophets proceeded from the commands of God. The prophets lived in these commands and, unlike the false spirits and teachers of human doctrine, they brought out no new teaching at all. Against the new teachings they cry and struggle the hardest, so that the people might remain with the commandments and the pure and clear Word of God and so that false teachings and other errors might always be prevented.

PSALM 31

For the director of music. A psalm of David.

In you, O Lord, I have taken refuge; let me never be put to shame; deliver me in your righteousness. Turn your ear to me, come quickly to my rescue; be my rock of refuge, a strong fortress to save me. Since you are my rock and my fortress, for the sake of your name lead and guide me. Free me from the trap that is set for me, for you are my refuge. Into your hands I commit my spirit; redeem me, O Lord, the God of truth.

I hate those who cling to worthless idols; I trust in the Lord. I will be glad and rejoice in your love, for you saw my affliction and knew the anguish of my soul. You have not handed me over to the enemy but have set my feet in a spacious place.

Be merciful to me, O Lord, for I am in distress; my eyes grow weak with sorrow, my soul and my body with grief. My life is consumed by anguish and my years by groaning; my strength fails because of my affliction, and my bones grow weak. Because of all my enemies, I am the utter contempt of my neighbors; I am a dread to my friends— those who see me on the street flee from me. I am forgotten by them as though I were dead; I have become like broken pottery. For I hear the slander of many; there is terror on every side; they conspire against me and plot to take my life.

But I trust in you, O Lord; I say, "You are my God." My times are in your hands; deliver me from my enemies and from those who pursue me.

Let your face shine on your servant; save me in your unfailing love. Let me not be put to shame, O Lord, for I have cried out to you; but let the wicked be put to shame and lie silent in the grave. Let their lying lips be silenced, for with pride and contempt they speak arrogantly against the righteous.

How great is your goodness, which you have stored up for those who fear you, which you bestow in the sight of men on those who take refuge in you. In the shelter of your presence you hide them from the intrigues of men; in your dwelling you keep them safe from accusing tongues.

Praise be to the Lord, for he showed his wonderful love to me when I was in a besieged city. In my alarm I said, "I am cut off from your sight!" Yet you heard my cry for mercy when I called to you for help.

Love the Lord, all his saints! The Lord preserves the faithful, but the proud he pays back in full. Be strong and take heart, all you who hope in the Lord.

PSALM 32

The 32nd psalm is an exemplary psalm of instruction which teaches us what sin is, how one might be freed from it and be righteous before God. For our reason does not know what sin is and tries to make satisfaction for it with works. But the psalmist says that even saints are sinners. They cannot become holy or blessed except by confessing themselves as sinners before God, knowing that they are regarded as righteous only from the grace of God, apart from any service or work.

In short, our righteousness is called (in plain language) the forgiveness of our sins. Or, as it says here: "sins not counted," "sins covered," "sins not to be seen." Here stand the clear plain words: all the saints are sinners and remain sinners. But they are holy because God in his grace neither sees nor counts these sins, but forgets, forgives, and covers them. There is thus no distinction between the saints and the nonsaints. They are sinners alike and all sin daily, only that the sins of the holy are not counted but covered; and the sins of the unholy are not covered but counted. One wound has a healing dressing on it and is bandaged; the other wound is open and unbandaged. Nevertheless, both of them are truly wounded, truly sinners, concerning which we in our books in other places have abundantly borne witness.

PSALM 32

Of David. A maskil.

Blessed is he whose transgressions are forgiven, whose sins are covered. Blessed is the man whose sin the Lord does not count against him and in whose spirit is no deceit.

When I kept silent, my bones wasted away through my groaning all day long. For day and night your hand was heavy upon me; my strength was sapped as in the heat of summer. Then I acknowledged my sin to you and did not cover up my iniquity. I said, ''I will confess my transgressions to the Lord''—and you forgave the guilt of my sin.

Therefore let everyone who is godly pray to you while you may be found; surely when the mighty waters rise, they will not reach him. You are my hiding place; you will protect me from trouble and surround me with songs of deliverance.

I will instruct you and teach you in the way you should go; I will counsel you and watch over you. Do not be like the horse or the mule, which have no understanding but must be controlled by bit and bridle or they will not come to you. Many are the woes of the wicked, but the Lord's unfailing love surrounds the man who trusts in him.

Rejoice in the Lord and be glad, you righteous; sing, all you who are upright in heart!

PSALM 33

The 33rd psalm is a psalm of thanks which thanks God in general for his blessings, for helping his faithful people in all kinds of distress and not letting them perish. He is able to help, since he made all things and still creates all things with a word, so that nothing is impossible with him. He is also so good and true that he will help and willingly helps, as he has promised in the first commandment: ''I will be your God,'' that is, I will be your comfort, help, salvation, life, and all good things, and I will stand against anything that would do you harm. That's what it means to "be God."

But the psalmist particularly thanks and praises the mighty blessing of God, that he guides the whole world, even the hearts, thoughts, intentions, anger, and fury of the kings and princes, not as they will, but as he wills. And he finally frustrates also all their intentions, so that they accomplish nothing as they really want. And what they intend to do against the righteous he immediately turns aside and overthrows. This is the particular joy and comfort of his saints against the arrogant and overweening insolence, the thrashing and threats of the raging nobles and the ruthless tyrants, who suppose that they can with threats devour all the saints of God and hurl God himself down from heaven. But before they have half begun, they lie in the dust. Consider the people of Sodom against Lot, Sennacherib the King, and our tyrants today—how totally countless intentions have been dashed up till now.

PSALM 33

Sing joyfully to the Lord, you righteous; it is fitting for the upright to praise him. Praise the Lord with the harp; make music to him on the ten-stringed lyre. Sing to him a new song; play skillfully, and shout for joy.

For the word of the Lord is right and true; he is faithful in all he does. The Lord loves righteousness and justice; the earth is full of his unfailing love.

By the word of the Lord were the heavens made, their starry host by the breath of his mouth. He gathers the waters of the sea into jars; he puts the deep into storehouses. Let all the earth fear the Lord; let all the people of the world revere him. For he spoke, and it came to be; he commanded, and it stood firm. The Lord foils the plans of the nations; he thwarts the purposes of the peoples. But the plans of the Lord stand firm forever, the purposes of his heart through all generations.

Blessed is the nation whose God is the Lord, the people he chose for his inheritance. From heaven the Lord looks down and sees all

mankind; from his dwelling place he watches all who live on earth—
he who forms the hearts of all, who considers everything they do.
No king is saved by the size of his army; no warrior escapes by his
great strength. A horse is a vain hope for deliverance; despite all its
great strength it cannot save. But the eyes of the Lord are on those
who fear him, on those whose hope is in his unfailing love, to deliver
them from death and keep them alive in famine.

We wait in hope for the Lord; he is our help and our shield. In him
our hearts rejoice, for we trust in his holy name. May your unfailing
love rest upon us, O Lord, even as we put our hope in you.

PSALM 34

The 34th psalm is a psalm of thanks. It is of much the same character
as the preceding psalm. It offers us the history of David as an example for all the righteous so that we might learn from him that God
never despises the cries of his saints. Moreover it teaches us to fear
God and no one else; further, to be on our guard against false teachers, against curses, grumblings, and slander. Rather, we should have
patience, bless enemies rather than curse them, wish them all good
and do good to them rather than evil, and so (as much as in us lies)
to live at peace with all people, whether they are evil or godly. For
it is certain (he says) that the righteous will suffer many things. It
cannot be otherwise. If you will be righteous, you must take up your
cross and suffer. This is how it must be.

On the other hand, it is certain that the Lord will truly help us out
of all these afflictions, that none of the least of your bones will be
taken away or missing. Yes, even the hairs of the head are numbered.
Although the bones of the saints in their martyrdom were often
broken, some of them burnt to ashes, and many more decaying in
their graves, they will yet return and not remain eternally broken or
be called broken. Rather, for a time they will be broken, but afterwards they will all again be more whole and healthy than they
formerly were.

This is the first psalm that speaks about angels and that they attend to the righteous and wait on us. They are not simply with us or around us. They are like an army—armed soldiers encamped around us, pitching their tents, keeping watch, and fighting for us against the devil and all his minions. This is a great and excellent comfort for all who believe, as the prophet Elisha, following this verse, made clear with his clear and correct example (2 Kings 6:17). But this verse is taken from Gen. 32:1–2, where the angels encounter the patriarch Jacob, because of which he called that city "army" or "camp." For they were his troops and camped around him as a protection, as the psalm here states.

PSALM 34

Of David. When he pretended to be insane before Abimelech, who drove him away, and he left.

I will extol the Lord at all times; his praise will always be on my lips. My soul will boast in the Lord; let the afflicted hear and rejoice. Glorify the Lord with me; let us exalt his name together.

I sought the Lord, and he answered me; he delivered me from all my fears. Those who look to him are radiant; their faces are never covered with shame. This poor man called, and the Lord heard him; he saved him out of all his troubles. The angel of the Lord encamps around those who fear him, and he delivers them.

Taste and see that the Lord is good; blessed is the man who takes refuge in him. Fear the Lord, you his saints, for those who fear him lack nothing. The lions may grow weak and hungry, but those who seek the Lord lack no good thing.

Come, my children, listen to me; I will teach you the fear of the Lord. Whoever of you loves life and desires to see many good days, keep your tongue from evil and your lips from speaking lies. Turn from evil and do good; seek peace and pursue it.

The eyes of the Lord are on the righteous and his ears are attentive to their cry; the face of the Lord is against those who do evil, to cut off the memory of them from the earth.

The righteous cry out, and the Lord hears them; he delivers them from all their troubles. The Lord is close to the brokenhearted and saves those who are crushed in spirit.

A righteous man may have many troubles, but the Lord delivers him from them all; he protects all his bones, not one of them will be broken.

Evil will slay the wicked; the foes of the righteous will be condemned. The Lord redeems his servants; no one will be condemned who takes refuge in him.

PSALM 35

The 35th psalm is a psalm of prayer in which David cries out against the shameful people who, for the sake of their enjoyment and profit, put up a pretense and say what the rulers would gladly hear. They defame the innocent, embittering the rulers against them and inciting them to violence. They devour the truth and cause great heartache. This happened to David, under Saul his king, when those whom he had treated well often afflicted him out of their own malice.

We take this as an example for our own time, when—both in sermons and in books, by the princes and in every place—our Gospel is so shamefully defamed with great lies beyond measure. And this is done, for the most part, by those whom we have served with all due honor and respect. Thus, they ascend and are praised, while we are overthrown and descend to the ground. This shameful, thankless, evil filthiness is nothing but the abominable belly with its servants.

In short, it happens (as Christ said of his betrayer) that "he who eats my bread betrays me with his feet"—and does so for thirty pieces of silver. Such are the hypocrites, who for the sake of food will devour the righteous, as David here cries.

PSALM 35

Of David.

Contend, O Lord, with those who contend with me; fight against those who fight against me. Take up shield and buckler; arise and come to my aid. Brandish spear and javelin against those who pursue me. Say to my soul, "I am your salvation."

May those who seek my life be disgraced and put to shame; may those who plot my ruin be turned back in dismay. May they be like chaff before the wind, with the angel of the Lord driving them away; may their path be dark and slippery, with the angel of the Lord pursuing them. Since they hid their net for me without cause and without cause dug a pit for me, may ruin overtake them by surprise— may the net they hid entangle them, may they fall into the pit, to their ruin. Then my soul will rejoice in the Lord and delight in his salvation. My whole being will exclaim, "Who is like you, O Lord? You rescue the poor from those too strong for them, the poor and needy from those who rob them."

Ruthless witnesses come forward; they question me on things I know nothing about. They repay me evil for good and leave my soul forlorn. Yet when they were ill, I put on sackcloth and humbled myself with fasting. When my prayers returned to me unanswered, I went about mourning as though for my friend or brother, I bowed my head in grief as though weeping for my mother. But when I stumbled, they gathered in glee; attackers gathered against me when I was unaware. They slandered me without ceasing. Like the ungodly they maliciously mocked; they gnashed their teeth at me. O Lord, how long will you look on? Rescue my life from their ravages, my precious life from these lions. I will give you thanks in the great assembly; among throngs of people I will praise you.

Let not those gloat over me who are my enemies without cause; let not those who hate me without reason maliciously wink the eye. They do not speak peaceably, but devise false accusations against those who live quietly in the land. They gape at me and say, "Aha! Aha! With our own eyes we have seen it."

O Lord, you have seen this; be not silent. Do not be far from me, O Lord. Awake, and rise to my defense! Contend for me, my God and Lord. Vindicate me in your righteousness, O Lord my God; do not let them gloat over me. Do not let them think "Aha, just what we wanted!" or say, "We have swallowed him up."

May all who gloat over my distress be put to shame and confusion; may all who exalt themselves over me be clothed with shame and disgrace. May those who delight in my vindication shout for joy and gladness; may they always say, "The Lord be exalted, who delights in the well-being of his servant." My tongue will speak of your righteousness and of your praises all day long.

PSALM 36

The 36th psalm is a psalm of instruction which warns us that we should be on guard against the false teachers, heretics, and rebellious spirits. These things the psalmist prays for at the end. In the middle of the psalm he gives us comfort as well, that despite everything, God's Word and kingdom will not be overthrown by means of their rabble. Instead it will stand in all the world like a mountain that the Lord himself establishes and like the deepest abyss that can be scooped out. The living and comforting Word shall thus remain in the house of God.

He portrays this masterfully saying: They are an evil venomous people who, in the first place, receive God's Word with total scorn and have no reverence for God at all. They are proud, impudent, and self-secure, teaching whatever they please. Second, they do not praise or honor God but honor themselves, while they slander all other teachers and bitterly revile them. In this they are masters, adorning themselves alone. Nowhere else is there any Spirit, any God, any church. Third, their doctrine is noxious, nothing but lies with which they contend against the faith and doctrine of grace. They deceive the people with their false brilliance and their lies. In the fourth place, they are rigid and stiff necked, tolerating neither instruction nor admonishment. Their head is harder than any anvil. Yes, when they see that someone reproves them rather than praising them, they burn and rage as the devil himself. In the fifth place, they continually push on and increase, expanding their domain, as St. Paul says (2 Tim. 2:17), "like a cancer." For they promote their doctrine ten times more strongly and more diligently than the true teachers do, as if they would overturn everything in one day. There is no day off or holiday with them. Finally, whenever possible they pursue and torment all those who do not go along with them, and they do this without dread, but with total audacity and confidence, as if they were doing God a service thereby.

PSALM 36

For the director of music. Of David the servant of the Lord.

An oracle is within my heart concerning the sinfulness of the wicked: There is no fear of God before his eyes. For in his own eyes he flatters himself too much to detect or hate his sin. The words of his mouth are wicked and deceitful; he has ceased to be wise and to do good. Even on his bed he plots evil; he commits himself to a sinful course and does not reject what is wrong.

Your love, O Lord, reaches to the heavens, your faithfulness to the skies. Your righteousness is like the mighty mountains, your justice like the great deep. O Lord, you preserve both man and beast. How priceless is your unfailing love! Both high and low among men find refuge in the shadow of your wings. They feast on the abundance of your house; you give them drink from your river of delights. For with you is the fountain of life; in your light we see light.

Continue your love to those who know you, your righteousness to the upright in heart. May the foot of the proud not come against me, nor the hand of the wicked drive me away. See how the evildoers lie fallen—thrown down, not able to rise!

PSALM 37

The 37th psalm is a psalm of comfort which teaches and exhorts us to have patience in the world and warns us, especially, against envy. For it is vexing and painful to the weak in faith when things go so well for the godless and the opposite happens to those who fear God. It is a great spiritual virtue when—seeing the great misdeeds of the peasants, the townspeople, the nobility, the princes, and everyone who has any power—one yet exerts himself not to blaspheme or inwardly wish this and that curse on them. Moreover, he still suffers and sees that all things go well for them and they remain unpunished.

Indeed, they are praised and honored, while the God-fearing are miserable, despised, hated, begrudged, obstructed, vexed, and persecuted.

The message is: Learn to have endurance. Take your heart to God and do not let yourself be vexed, do not become envious, or curse, or wish evil to fall, or murmur, or look at them with hatred. Let these people go and commend them to God, who will surely find all things out. The psalm teaches this and comforts us in a variety of ways, with abundant promises, with examples, with warnings. For it is a great and difficult art to manifest such patient long-suffering, when reason and all the heathen count envy as virtue. For it appears as though it were just and fair to envy and begrudge the ungodly for their wantonness, their good fortune, and their riches.

PSALM 37

Of David.

Do not fret because of evil men or be envious of those who do wrong; for like the grass they will soon wither, like green plants they will soon die away.

Trust in the Lord and do good; dwell in the land and enjoy safe pasture. Delight yourself in the Lord and he will give you the desires of your heart.

Commit your way to the Lord; trust in him and he will do this: He will make your righteousness shine like the dawn, the justice of your cause like the noonday sun.

Be still before the Lord and wait patiently for him; do not fret when men succeed in their ways, when they carry out their wicked schemes.

Refrain from anger and turn from wrath; do not fret—it leads only to evil. For evil men will be cut off, but those who hope in the Lord will inherit the land.

A little while, and the wicked will be no more; though you look for them, they will not be found. But the meek will inherit the land and enjoy great peace.

The wicked plot against the righteous and gnash their teeth at them; but the Lord laughs at the wicked, for he knows their day is coming.

The wicked draw the sword and bend the bow to bring down the poor and needy, to slay those whose ways are upright. But their swords will pierce their own hearts, and their bows will be broken.

Better the little that the righteous have than the wealth of many wicked; for the power of the wicked will be broken, but the Lord upholds the righteous.

The days of the blameless are known to the Lord, and their inheritance will endure forever. In times of disaster they will not wither; in days of famine they will enjoy plenty.

But the wicked will perish: The Lord's enemies will be like the beauty of the fields, they will vanish—vanish like smoke.

The wicked borrow and do not repay, but the righteous give generously; those the Lord blesses will inherit the land, but those he curses will be cut off.

If the Lord delights in a man's way, he makes his steps firm; though he stumble, he will not fall, for the Lord upholds him with his hand.

I was young and now I am old, yet I have never seen the righteous forsaken or their children begging bread. They are always generous and lend freely; their children will be blessed.

Turn from evil and do good; then you will dwell in the land forever. For the Lord loves the just and will not forsake his faithful ones.

They will be protected forever, but the offspring of the wicked will be cut off; the righteous will inherit the land and dwell in it forever.

The mouth of the righteous man utters wisdom, and his tongue speaks what is just. The law of his God is in his heart; his feet do not slip.

The wicked lie in wait for the righteous, seeking their very lives; but the Lord will not leave them in their power or let them be condemned when brought to trial.

Wait for the Lord and keep his way. He will exalt you to inherit the land; when the wicked are cut off, you will see it.

I have seen a wicked and ruthless man flourishing like a green tree in its native soil, but he soon passed away and was no more; though I looked for him, he could not be found.

Consider the blameless, observe the upright; there is a future for the man of peace. But all sinners will be destroyed; the future of the wicked will be cut off.

The salvation of the righteous comes from the Lord; he is their stronghold in time of trouble. The Lord helps them and delivers them; he delivers them from the wicked and saves them, because they take refuge in him.

PSALM 38

The 38th psalm is a psalm of prayer in which the psalmist laments over his sins, on account of which his conscience despairs and is greatly afflicted and can see nothing but God's arrows, that is, God's anger, threats, death, and hell. These sorrows consume marrow and bone, strength and fluids. They disfigure the appearance and the complexion and alter one's total understanding and demeanor. For to truly feel one's sins and despair over a guilty conscience is the torture above all torture. Moreover, outward persecutors add to this "comfort," pursuing the righteous in their conscience and boasting that God is with them and against the righteous. And since God here holds back his comfort, this terror in the heart follows, that God is angry with them on account of their sins.

But for all that, the psalmist teaches us to hold fast and not despair. He teaches us to arm ourselves with prayer against their boasts, to lay claim to God's promise and take hold of it to the proper end, namely that we be godly and righteous before God. Then the comfort of faith will flow again. Likewise, we too should pray and not despair in any anxiety, although we are sinners and feel sharply the burden and assault of our sins.

PSALM 38

A psalm of David. A petition.

O Lord, do not rebuke me in your anger or discipline me in your wrath. For your arrows have pierced me, and your hand has come down upon me. Because of your wrath there is no health in my body; my bones have no soundness because of my sin. My guilt has overwhelmed me like a burden too heavy to bear.

My wounds fester and are loathsome because of my sinful folly. I am bowed down and brought very low; all day long I go about mourning. My back is filled with searing pain; there is no health in my body. I am feeble and utterly crushed; I groan in anguish of heart.

All my longings lie open before you, O Lord; my sighing is not hidden from you. My heart pounds, my strength fails me; even the light has gone from my eyes. My friends and companions avoid me because of my wounds; my neighbors stay far away. Those who seek my life set their traps, those who would harm me talk of my ruin; all day long they plot deception.

I am like a deaf man, who cannot hear, like a mute, who cannot open his mouth; I have become like a man who does not hear, whose mouth can offer no reply. I wait for you, O Lord; you will answer, O Lord my God. For I said, ''Do not let them gloat or exalt themselves over me when my foot slips.''

For I am about to fall, and my pain is ever with me. I confess my iniquity; I am troubled by my sin. Many are those who are my vigorous enemies; those who hate me without reason are numerous. Those who repay my good with evil slander me when I pursue what is good.

O Lord, do not forsake me; be not far from me, O my God. Come quickly to help me, O Lord my Savior.

PSALM 39

The 39th psalm is a psalm of comfort. The psalmist prays that God not let him murmer or become impatient because the godless live securely and accumulate goods as if they would never die, while the godly are constantly plagued and punished on account of their sins. He desires rather that God would grant him to think of how short and uncertain this life is, lest he join the ungodly and live without fear of death in careless greed and vain display.

For it is a great vexation which troubles many hearts that the evil live so confidently in riotous living, but the godly are troubled and in misery. But, in the end, we find that the best of all is still to have the forgiveness of sins and a gracious God, who will help us out of any misery, as the psalm here says and prays.

PSALM 39

For the director of music. For Jeduthun. A psalm of David.

I said, "I will watch my ways and keep my tongue from sin; I will put a muzzle on my mouth as long as the wicked are in my presence." But when I was silent and still, not even saying anything good, my anguish increased. My heart grew hot within me, and as I meditated, the fire burned; then I spoke with my tongue:

"Show me, O Lord, my life's end and the number of my days; let me know how fleeting is my life. You have made my days a mere handbreadth; the span of my years is as nothing before you. Each man's life is but a breath. Man is a mere phantom as he goes to and fro: He bustles about, but only in vain; he heaps up wealth, not knowing who will get it.

"But now, Lord, what do I look for? My hope is in you. Save me from all my transgressions; do not make me the scorn of fools. I was silent; I would not open my mouth, for you are the one who has done this. Remove your scourge from me; I am overcome by the blow of your hand. You rebuke and discipline men for their sin; you consume their wealth like a moth—each man is but a breath.

"Hear my prayer, O Lord, listen to my cry for help; be not deaf to my weeping. For I dwell with you as an alien, a stranger, as all my fathers were. Look away from me, that I may rejoice again before I depart and am no more."

PSALM 40

The 40th psalm is a beautiful psalm of prayer in which Christ himself laments his sufferings and calls for rescue from death. It clearly prophesies that he alone does God's will and fulfills the law, and that this is written about him in the book of Moses. He dissolves and abolishes the old law of sacrifices and its holiness by which God's will was not fulfilled. Everything is done for us by God himself alone, not by our work or sacrifices. He therefore promises and establishes the New Testament in which the justification of the believers will be preached in the great congregation, that is, in the entire world, and not the justification by sacrifices or our works. For works and sacrifices make only arrogant and false saints whose hope lies not in God nor in his grace, but in their lies and false holiness.

PSALM 40

For the director of music. Of David. A psalm.

I waited patiently for the Lord; he turned to me and heard my cry. He lifted me out of the slimy pit, out of the mud and mire; he set my feet on a rock and gave me a firm place to stand. He put a new song in my mouth, a hymn of praise to our God. Many will see and fear and put their trust in the Lord.

Blessed is the man who makes the Lord his trust, who does not look to the proud, to those who turn aside to false gods. Many, O Lord my God, are the wonders you have done. The things you planned for us no one can recount to you; were I to speak and tell of them, they would be too many to declare.

Sacrifice and offering you did not desire, but my ears you have pierced; burnt offerings and sin offerings you did not require. Then I said, "Here I am, I have come—it is written about me in the scroll. I desire to do your will, O my God; your law is within my heart."

I proclaim righteousness in the great assembly; I do not seal my lips, as you know, O Lord. I do not hide your righteousness in my heart; I speak of your faithfulness and salvation. I do not conceal your love and your truth from the great assembly.

Do not withhold your mercy from me, O Lord; may your love and your truth always protect me. For troubles without number surround me; my sins have overtaken me, and I cannot see. They are more than the hairs of my head, and my heart fails within me.

Be pleased, O Lord, to save me; O Lord, come quickly to help me. May all who seek to take my life be put to shame and confusion; may all who desire my ruin be turned back in disgrace. May those who say to me, ''Aha! Aha!'' be appalled at their own shame. But may all who seek you rejoice and be glad in you; may those who love your salvation always say, ''The Lord be exalted!''

Yet I am poor and needy; may the Lord think of me. You are my help and my deliverer; O my God, do not delay.

PSALM 41

The 41st psalm is a psalm of prayer in which Christ himself prophesies and laments over his betrayer, Judas, together with his comrades, by whom he would be crucified. He prays that he would be raised up from death and that he might be elevated to God's presence at his right hand. But he offers comfort for the multitudes by making himself into a sinner, though truly he was without any sin. Thus he stands and declares himself to be in our place, in our person, and he carries our sins as if they were his own, as if he had committed them himself.

However, in the beginning of the psalm, he declares a blessing for those who show regard for those in misery, that is, those who do not become offended at Jesus Christ, the miserable crucified sinner, but hold fast to him. For it is very offensive to believe that such a poor condemned sinner should be raised so high that he may sit at the right hand of God.

PSALM 41

For the director of music. A psalm of David.

Blessed is he who has regard for the weak; the Lord delivers him in times of trouble. The Lord will protect him and preserve his life; he will bless him in the land and not surrender him to the desire of his foes. The Lord will sustain him on his sickbed and restore him from his bed of illness.

I said, "O Lord, have mercy on me; heal me, for I have sinned against you." My enemies say of me in malice, "When will he die and his name perish?" Whenever one comes to see me, he speaks falsely, while his heart gathers slander; then he goes out and spreads it abroad.

All my enemies whisper together against me; they imagine the worst for me, saying, "A vile disease has beset him; he will never get up from the place where he lies." Even my close friend, whom I trusted, he who shared my bread, has lifted up his heel against me.

But you, O Lord, have mercy on me; raise me up, that I may repay them. I know that you are pleased with me, for my enemy does not triumph over me. In my integrity you uphold me and set me in your presence forever.

Praise be to the Lord, the God of Israel, from everlasting to everlasting. Amen and Amen.

PSALM 42

The 42nd psalm is a psalm of prayer in which the psalmist laments over his sorrows of heart, that God was angry with him and had afflicted him. Because of these he is mocked by the godless who say, "Where is your God now?" For the godless cannot restrain themselves; when they see that things go ill with the godly, they whistle, laugh, and wink: "Ah, how rightly this comes to pass!" So they say, "This is what happens to the heretics." When someone else is troubled, they know nothing else than that it is a sure sign of God's anger. But when they are troubled, then it can have no other meaning than that they are suffering for God's sake and they must be God's holy martyrs. These wrongheaded, blind, and poisonous guides for the blind will not understand that God flogs his own people, yet comforts them again and does not desert them. The psalmist on the other hand desires to come to God's house and be comforted by the face of God. That is, he wants to truly hear God's

Word, which comforts him. For God's house is that place where God's Word is, and God's face is his presence, through which he makes himself known and by means of his Word, reveals his grace. Elsewhere in the Scripture (Jer. 2:27), it says, "Turn not your back, but your face toward us."

PSALM 42

For the director of music. A maskil *of the Sons of Korah.*

As the deer pants for streams of water, so my soul pants for you, O God. My soul thirsts for God, for the living God. When can I go and meet with God? My tears have been my food day and night, while men say to me all day long, "Where is your God?" These things I remember as I pour out my soul: how I used to go with the multitude, leading the procession to the house of God, with shouts of joy and thanksgiving among the festive throng.

Why are you downcast, O my soul? Why so disturbed within me? Put your hope in God, for I will yet praise him, my Savior and my God.

My soul is downcast within me; therefore I will remember you from the land of the Jordan, the heights of Hermon—from Mount Mizar. Deep calls to deep in the roar of your waterfalls; all your waves and breakers have swept over me.

By day the Lord directs his love, at night his song is with me—a prayer to the God of my life.

I say to God my Rock, "Why have you forgotten me? Why must I go about mourning, oppressed by the enemy?"

My bones suffer mortal agony as my foes taunt me, saying to me all day long, "Where is your God?"

Why are you downcast, O my soul? Why so disturbed within me? Put your hope in God, for I will yet praise him, my Savior and my God.

PSALM 43

The 43rd psalm is similar to the preceding psalm and has nearly the same words in it. For he desires also by light and truth to come to God's house, that is, to be comforted in his misery by God's Word.

PSALM 43

Vindicate me, O God, and plead my cause against an ungodly nation; rescue me from deceitful and wicked men. You are God my stronghold. Why have you rejected me? Why must I go about mourning, oppressed by the enemy? Send forth your light and your truth, let them guide me; let them bring me to your holy mountain, to the place where you dwell. Then will I go to the altar of God, to God, my joy and my delight. I will praise you with the harp, O God, my God.

Why are you downcast, O my soul? Why so disturbed within me? Put your hope in God, for I will yet praise him, my Savior and my God.

PSALM 44

The 44th psalm is a general psalm of prayer in which all the saints, especially the New Testament saints, lament that they are persecuted by the heathen and tyrants and would be slaughtered. They cry out that God has given them over to this, as if he had abandoned them. Formerly he had helped them with great wonders, and no harm came to them from persecutions. But they are now even persecuted on their own account, that is, for God's sake, as if they had done all kinds evil. In summary, this psalm is the sighing of the Spirit. It rebukes the flesh, which murmurs against God that it is judged unrighteous and is so poorly governed (according to reason) that the godly, who ought to be helped, are allowed to suffer, and the evil, who ought to be punished, are elevated.

For the director of music. Of the Sons of Korah. A maskil.

We have heard with our ears, O God; our fathers have told us what you did in their days, in days long ago. With your hand you drove out the nations and planted our fathers; you crushed the peoples and made our fathers flourish. It was not by their sword that they won the land, nor did their arm bring them victory; it was your right hand, your arm, and the light of your face, for you loved them.

You are my King and my God, who decrees victories for Jacob. Through you we push back our enemies; through your name we trample our foes. I do not trust in my bow, my sword does not bring me victory; but you give us victory over our enemies, you put our adversaries to shame. In God we make our boast all day long, and we will praise your name forever.

But now you have rejected and humbled us; you no longer go out with our armies. You made us retreat before the enemy, and our adversaries have plundered us. You gave us up to be devoured like sheep and have scattered us among the nations. You sold your people for a pittance, gaining nothing from their sale.

You have made us a reproach to our neighbors, the scorn and derision of those around us. You have made us a byword among the nations; the peoples shake their heads at us. My disgrace is before me all day long, and my face is covered with shame at the taunts of those who reproach and revile me, because of the enemy, who is bent on revenge.

All this happened to us, though we had not forgotten you or been false to your covenant. Our hearts had not turned back; our feet had not strayed from your path. But you crushed us and made us a haunt for jackals and covered us over with deep darkness.

If we had forgotten the name of our God or spread out our hands to a foreign god, would not God have discovered it, since he knows the secrets of the heart? Yet for your sake we face death all day long; we are considered as sheep to be slaughtered.

rd! Why do you sleep? Rouse yourself! Do not reject
ver. Why do you hide your face and forget our misery and
oppression?

We are brought down to the dust; our bodies cling to the ground.
Rise up and help us; redeem us because of your unfailing love.

PSALM 45

The 45th psalm is a prophecy of the Gospel and the kingdom of
Christ, adorned with magnificent, splendid, and powerful words.
For it portrays Christ as a king—with all kingly splendor, very
handsome, well spoken, well adorned, well armored, successful in
war, righteous, gentle, gracious, having likewise a fine castle, a
grand host of ladies-in-waiting, a beautiful queen and children forever. This all is nothing else than a spiritual picture of the Gospel
of Christ, his Spirit, grace, church, and eternal life, of war against
sin, death, law, devil, flesh, world, and all evil.

The psalm also clearly proclaims that the Old Testament shall come
to an end. For it calls on the daughters to forget their father's house
and people and call on this king as the one God, of which there is
no other God. It gives him also the honor of the first commandment,
namely prayer, and it names him clearly as the true God, acknowl-
edging him to be the eternal king who rules in righteousness and
takes sin away. An eternal king can only be God himself. This is
however not the time to speak further of these things.

PSALM 45

*For the director of music. To the tune of "Lilies." Of the Sons of
Korah. A maskil. A wedding song.*

My heart is stirred by a noble theme as I recite my verses for the
king; my tongue is the pen of a skillful writer.

You are the most excellent of men and your lips have been anointed
with grace, since God has blessed you forever. Gird your sword
upon your side, O mighty one; clothe yourself with splendor and

majesty. In your majesty ride forth victoriously in behalf of truth, humility and righteousness; let your right hand display awesome deeds. Let your sharp arrows pierce the hearts of the king's enemies; let the nations fall beneath your feet. Your throne, O God, will last for ever and ever; a scepter of justice will be the scepter of your kingdom. You love righteousness and hate wickedness; therefore God, your God, has set you above your companions by anointing you with the oil of joy. All your robes are fragrant with myrrh and aloes and cassia; from palaces adorned with ivory the music of the strings makes you glad. Daughters of kings are among your honored women; at your right hand is the royal bride in gold of Ophir.

Listen, O daughter, consider and give ear: Forget your people and your father's house. The king is enthralled by your beauty; honor him, for he is your lord. The Daughter of Tyre will come with a gift, men of wealth will seek your favor.

All glorious is the princess within her chamber; her gown is interwoven with gold. In embroidered garments she is led to the king; her virgin companions follow her and are brought to you. They are led in with joy and gladness; they enter the palace of the king.

Your sons will take the place of your fathers; you will make them princes throughout the land. I will perpetuate your memory through all generations; therefore the nations will praise you for ever and ever.

PSALM 46

The 46th psalm is a psalm of thanks, sung by the people of Israel because of the mighty deeds of God. He had protected and saved the city of Jerusalem, in which was his dwelling, against all the rage and the fury of all the kings and the nations and preserved their peace against all warfare and weapons. And, in the manner of the Scriptures, the psalm calls the character of the city a "little spring of water," that is, a little stream that shall not run dry, as opposed to the great rivers, seas, and oceans of the heathen—their great kingdoms, principalities, and domains—that shall dry up and disappear.

We, on the other hand, sing this psalm [the basis of Luther's hymn "A Mighty Fortress"] to praise God for being with us. He miraculously preserves his Word and Christendom against the gates of hell, against the rage of the devil, the rebellious spirits, the world, the flesh, sin, death. Our little spring of water also is a living fountain, while their puddles, pools, and ponds become foul, malodorous, and dry.

PSALM 46

For the director of music. Of the Sons of Korah. According to alamoth. *A song.*

God is our refuge and strength, an ever-present help in trouble. Therefore we will not fear, though the earth give way and the mountains fall into the heart of the sea, though its waters roar and foam and the mountains quake with their surging.

There is a river whose streams make glad the city of God, the holy place where the Most High dwells. God is within her, she will not fall; God will help her at break of day. Nations are in uproar, kingdoms fall; he lifts his voice, the earth melts.

The Lord Almighty is with us; the God of Jacob is our fortress.

Come and see the works of the Lord, the desolations he has brought on the earth. He makes wars cease to the ends of the earth; he breaks the bow and shatters the spear, he burns the shields with fire. "Be still, and know that I am God; I will be exalted among the nations, I will be exalted in the earth."

The Lord Almighty is with us; the God of Jacob is our fortress.

PSALM 47

The 47th psalm is a prophecy of Christ, that he shall rise up and become king over all the world, without a battle, simply through shouts, songs, and trumpet calls, that is, through the joyful preaching of the Gospel, just as the walls of Jericho fell by trumpet blasts and shouts, without any weapons at all.

PSALM 47

For the director of music. Of the Sons of Korah. A psalm.

Clap your hands, all you nations; shout to God with cries of joy. How awesome is the Lord Most High, the great King over all the earth! He subdued nations under us, peoples under our feet. He chose our inheritance for us, the pride of Jacob, whom he loved.

God has ascended amid shouts of joy, the Lord amid the sounding of trumpets. Sing praises to God, sing praises; sing praises to our King, sing praises.

For God is the King of all the earth; sing to him a psalm of praise. God reigns over the nations; God is seated on his holy throne. The nobles of the nations assemble as the people of the God of Abraham, for the kings of the earth belong to God; he is greatly exalted.

PSALM 48

The 48th psalm is a psalm of thanks, very much like the 46th psalm. It also praises God for protecting and defending the city of Jerusalem against the kings and princes. They had to retreat in shame and let the temple stand, along with the worship of God and his Word (or rule). With this God has kept his promise, namely, that in accordance with the first commandment, he would be their God. For, the psalm says, what we have heard and believed, we also see and experience in God's actions for the city.

We also sing this psalm for Christendom and the Gospel, that they will stand against the raging of the kings and princes, who finally withdraw in shame—and the Word they still must let remain.

PSALM 48

A song. A psalm of the Sons of Korah.

Great is the Lord, and most worthy of praise, in the city of our God, his holy mountain. It is beautiful in its loftiness, the joy of the whole earth. Like the utmost heights of Zaphon is Mount Zion, the city of the Great King. God is in her citadels; he has shown himself to be her fortress.

When the kings joined forces, when they advanced together, they saw her and were astounded; they fled in terror. Trembling seized them there, pain like that of a woman in labor. You destroyed them like ships of Tarshish shattered by an east wind.

As we have heard, so have we seen in the city of the Lord Almighty, in the city of our God: God makes her secure forever.

Within your temple, O God, we meditate on your unfailing love. Like your name, O God, your praise reaches to the ends of the earth; your right hand is filled with righteousness. Mount Zion rejoices, the villages of Judah are glad because of your judgments.

Walk about Zion, go around her, count her towers, consider well her ramparts, view her citadels, that you may tell of them to the next generation. For this God is our God for ever and ever; he will be our guide even to the end.

PSALM 49

The 49th psalm is a psalm of instruction against the great god of the world, Mammon by name. It rebukes as great fools those who trust in his rule and do not see that he cannot deliver them—or himself—from death. Therefore it is truly better to rely on God, who delivers from death and gives eternal life, while they perish like the beasts and leave all their goods behind, not knowing who will obtain it all.

PSALM 49

For the director of music. Of the Sons of Korah. A psalm.

Hear this, all you peoples; listen, all who live in this world, both low and high, rich and poor alike: My mouth will speak words of wisdom; the utterance from my heart will give understanding. I will turn my ear to a proverb; with the harp I will expound my riddle:

Why should I fear when evil days come, when wicked deceivers surround me—those who trust in their wealth and boast of their great riches? No man can redeem the life of another or give to God a ransom for him—the ransom for a life is costly, no payment is ever enough—that he should live on forever and not see decay.

For all can see that wise men die; the foolish and the senseless alike perish and leave their wealth to others. Their tombs will remain their houses forever, their dwellings for endless generations, though they had named lands after themselves.

But man, despite his riches, does not endure; he is like the beasts that perish.

This is the fate of those who trust in themselves, and of their followers, who approve their sayings. Like sheep they are destined for the grave, and death will feed on them. The upright will rule over them in the morning; their forms will decay in the grave far from their princely mansions. But God will redeem my life from the grave; he will surely take me to himself.

Do not be overawed when a man grows rich, when the splendor of his house increases; for he will take nothing with him when he dies, his splendor will not descend with him. Though while he lived he counted himself blessed—and men praise you when you prosper— he will join the generation of his fathers, who will never see the light of life.

A man who has riches without understanding is like the beasts that perish.

PSALM 50

Psalm 50 is a psalm of instruction which tells us of the true worship of God and true sacrifice in contrast to the false saints. They value their own sacrifices and worship highly, as if God must surely be thankful and indebted to them. God however reverses this. He intends for his goodness and help to be so highly esteemed that we will be thankful and indebted to him.

Likewise, when the psalm commands that vows be fulfilled, this does not mean absurd self-chosen vows, but those that are commanded in the Ten Commandments, especially in the first and second—that we praise God, that we trust in him, call on him, praise and thank him as our only God, and the like. Of this, the raving saints and the hypocrites know nothing.

Mark well the clear words with which the psalm closes. The last verse teaches us that to call upon God in distress and thank him is the true worship, the most pleasing offering, and the right way to salvation.

PSALM 50

A psalm of Asaph.

The Mighty One, God, the Lord, speaks and summons the earth from the rising of the sun to the place where it sets. From Zion, perfect in beauty, God shines forth. Our God comes and will not be silent; a fire devours before him, and around him a tempest rages. He summons the heavens above, and the earth, that he may judge his people: "Gather to me my consecrated ones, who made a covenant with me by sacrifice." And the heavens proclaim his righteousness, for God himself is judge.

"Hear, O my people, and I will speak, O Israel, and I will testify against you: I am God, your God. I do not rebuke you for your sacrifices or your burnt offerings, which are ever before me. I have no need of a bull from your stall or of goats from your pens, for every animal of the forest is mine, and the cattle on a thousand hills. I know every bird in the mountains, and the creatures of the field are mine. If I were hungry I would not tell you, for the world is mine, and all that is in it. Do I eat the flesh of bulls or drink the blood of goats? Sacrifice thank offerings to God, fulfill your vows to the Most High, and call upon me in the day of trouble; I will deliver you, and you will honor me."

But to the wicked, God says: "What right have you to recite my laws or take my covenant on your lips? You hate my instruction and cast my words behind you. When you see a thief, you join with him; you throw in your lot with adulterers. You use your mouth for evil and harness your tongue to deceit. You speak continually against your brother and slander your own mother's son. These things you have done and I kept silent; you thought I was altogether like you. But I will rebuke you and accuse you to your face.

"Consider this, you who forget God, or I will tear you to pieces, with none to rescue: He who sacrifices thank offerings honors me, and he prepares the way so that I may show him the salvation of God."

PSALM 51

Psalm 51 is one of the foremost of the psalms of instruction. In it David truly teaches us what sin is, where it comes from, what damage it does—and how one may be freed from it. In this psalm, as nowhere else, it is clearly shown that sin is an inheritance, born in us, and that no works can help us against it, only God's grace and forgiveness. Through his Spirit, he creates us new again, as a new person, a new creation. Otherwise, says David, sin with its terror and despair is so mighty that it even crushes the bones, until God's grace comes to our comfort.

Afterwards, when by grace and the Spirit we have again become new, then we can not only learn how to praise but actually thank and praise God—yes, even suffer and bear the cross. All of this David calls true sacrifice and worship. He rejects all other sacrifices which the raving saints bring. He prays at the end that God might build up and preserve the city of Jerusalem to such sacrifices and worship.

PSALM 51

For the director of music. A psalm of David. When the prophet Nathan came to him after David had commited adultery with Bathsheba.

Have mercy on me, O God, according to your unfailing love; according to your great compassion blot out my transgressions. Wash away all my iniquity and cleanse me from my sin.

For I know my transgressions, and my sin is always before me. Against you, you only, have I sinned and done what is evil in your sight, so that you are proved right when you speak and justified when you judge. Surely I was sinful at birth, sinful from the time my mother conceived me. Surely you desire truth in the inner parts; you teach me wisdom in the inmost place.

Cleanse me with hyssop, and I will be clean; wash me, and I will be whiter than snow. Let me hear joy and gladness; let the bones you have crushed rejoice. Hide your face from my sins and blot out all my iniquity.

Create in me a pure heart, O God, and renew a steadfast spirit within me. Do not cast me from your presence or take your Holy Spirit from me. Restore to me the joy of your salvatiuon and grant me a willing spirit, to sustain me.

Then I will teach transgressors your ways, and sinners will turn back to you. Save me from bloodguilt, O God, the God who saves me, and my tongue will sing of your righteousness. O Lord, open my lips, and my mouth will declare your praise. You do not delight in sacrifice, or I would bring it; you do not take pleasure in burnt offerings. The sacrifices of God are a broken spirit; a broken and contrite heart, O God, you will not despise.

In your good pleasure make Zion prosper; build up the walls of Jerusalem. Then there will be righteous sacrifices, whole burnt offerings to delight you; then bulls will be offered on your altar.

PSALM 52

The 52nd psalm is a psalm of comfort. As the title shows, it speaks of Doeg, who betrayed David and shed much innocent blood (1 Samuel 22). He was a traitor and bloodthirsty dog, who slandered those who hope in God's Word he reviled God's servants and incited kings and princes to shed innocent blood. In spite of such malevolent people, this psalm brings comfort. It announces their reward, that they shall be removed from body, goods, house, and land. But the godly shall remain and retain God's house and his Word.

PSALM 52

For the director of music. A maskil *of David. When Doeg the Edom-ite had gone to Saul and told him: "David has gone to the house of Ahimelech."*

Why do you boast of evil, you mighty man? Why do you boast all day long, you who are a disgrace in the eyes of God? Your tongue plots destruction; it is like a sharpened razor, you who practice deceit. You love evil rather than good, falsehood rather than speaking the truth. You love every harmful word, O you deceitful tongue!

Surely God will bring you down to everlasting ruin: He will snatch you up and tear you from your tent; he will uproot you from the land of the living. The righteous will see and fear; they will laugh at him, saying, "Here now is the man who did not make God his stronghold but trusted in his great wealth and grew strong by destroying others!"

But I am like an olive tree flourishing in the house of God; I trust in God's unfailing love for ever and ever. I will praise you forever for what you have done; in your name I will hope, for your name is good. I will praise you in the presence of your saints.

PSALM 53

The 53rd psalm is a psalm of instruction and a prophecy, like the 14th psalm. Both have nearly the same verses and words. In brief, both of them rebuke the faithless work-saints, who persecute the true doctrine and the true teachers. At the end, it proclaims the Gospel and kingdom of Christ, who shall come out of Zion.

PSALM 53

For the director of music. According to mahalath. *A* maskil *of David.*

The fool says in his heart, "There is no God." They are corrupt, and their ways are vile; there is no one who does good.

God looks down from heaven on the sons of men to see if there are any who understand, any who seek God. Everyone has turned away, they have together become corrupt; there is no one who does good, not even one.

Will the evildoers never learn—those who devour my people as men eat bread and who do not call on God? There they were, overwhelmed with dread, where there was nothing to dread. God scattered the bones of those who attacked you; you put them to shame, for God despised them.

Oh, that salvation for Israel would come out of Zion! When God restores the fortunes of his people, let Jacob rejoice and Israel be glad!

PSALM 54

The 54th psalm is a psalm of prayer against the persecutors who seek the life of the godly on account of the Word of God. Thus Saul and those in Ziph had attempted to kill David on account of the Word of God, through which he had been called and consecrated to be king. He prays for deliverance from his enemies and vengeance upon them.

PSALM 54

For the director of music. With stringed instruments. A maskil *of David. When the Ziphites had gone to Saul and said, "Is not David hiding among us?"*

Save me, O God, by your name; vindicate me by your might. Hear my prayer, O God; listen to the words of my mouth.

Strangers are attacking me; ruthless men seek my life—men without regard for God.

Surely God is my help; the Lord is the one who sustains me.

Let evil recoil on those who slander me; in your faithfulness destroy them.

I will sacrifice a freewill offering to you; I will praise your name, O Lord, for it is good. For he has delivered me from all my troubles, and my eyes have looked in triumph on my foes.

PSALM 55

The 55th psalm is a psalm of prayer. Although it might have been spoken in the person of Christ against his betrayer, Judas, I rather let it remain a general prayer against those vile alleycats who lick in front and scratch in back. In appearance, they are such true friends, fathers, brothers, and sisters, so full of love and life compared to us, that their mouth is smoother than butter and oil. But behind the scene is nothing but murder, sword, warfare, and the destruction of all, as he says here. That is, they can go with us to the table, to church, in house, on the street and be the best of companions. Therefore he says that the devil or death and hell may carry them away, for they create a great heartache and affliction for the people. This curse however is a prophecy—thus it will certainly be with them, for they can say nothing better. Or rather, "They never change their ways and have no fear of God."

PSALM 55

For the director of music. With stringed instruments. A maskil *of David.*

Listen to my prayer, O God, do not ignore my plea; hear me and answer me. My thoughts trouble me and I am distraught at the voice of the enemy, at the stares of the wicked; for they bring down suffering upon me and revile me in their anger.

My heart is in anguish within me; the terrors of death assail me. Fear and trembling have beset me; horror has overwhelmed me. I said, "Oh, that I had the wings of a dove! I would fly away and be at rest—I would flee far away and stay in the desert; I would hurry to my place of shelter, far from the tempest and storm."

Confuse the wicked, O Lord, confound their speech, for I see violence and strife in the city. Day and night they prowl about on its walls; malice and abuse are within it. Destructive forces are at work in the city; threats and lies never leave its streets.

If an enemy were insulting me, I could endure it; if a foe were raising himself against me, I could hide from him. But it is you, a man like myself, my companion, my close friend, with whom I once enjoyed sweet fellowship as we walked with the throng at the house of God.

Let death take my enemies by surprise; let them go down alive to the grave, for evil finds lodging among them.

But I call to God, and the Lord saves me. Evening, morning and noon I cry out in distress, and he hears my voice. He ransoms me unharmed from the battle waged against me, even though many oppose me. God, who is enthroned forever, will hear them and afflict them—men who never change their ways and have no fear of God.

My companion attacks his friends; he violates his covenant. His speech is smooth as butter, yet war is in his heart; his words are more soothing than oil, yet they are drawn swords.

Cast your cares on the Lord and he will sustain you; he will never let the righteous fall. But you, O God, will bring down the wicked into the pit of corruption; bloodthirsty and deceitful men will not live out half their days.

But as for me, I trust in you.

PSALM 56

The 56th psalm is a psalm of prayer in which David laments over Saul and his men, who forced him to flee from them out of the land to the Philistines. They pressed him so hard that he had nowhere he could safely go. But he had this comfort, that he had God's Word and the promise and right of the kingship, though they daily assailed it and opposed or even denied it, saying that he shall never be king, but rather Saul and his heirs.

We pray this psalm against our tyrants, who ceaselessly persecute God's Word and us and allow no place for peace. But we also have this comfort, that we have God's Word on our behalf, though they daily oppose, assail, and speak against that Word, saying that we are heretics and they alone are the true church.

PSALM 56

For the director of music. To the tune of "A Dove on Distant Oaks." Of David. A miktam. *When the Philistines had seized him in Gath.*

Be merciful to me, O God, for men hotly pursue me; all day long they press their attack. My slanderers pursue me all day long; many are attacking me in their pride.

When I am afraid, I will trust in you. In God, whose word I praise, in God I trust; I will not be afraid. What can mortal man do to me?

All day long they twist my words; they are always plotting to harm me. They conspire, they lurk, they watch my steps, eager to take my life.

On no account let them escape; in your anger, O God, bring down the nations. Record my lament; list my tears on your scroll—are they not in your record?

Then my enemies will turn back when I call for help. By this I will know that God is for me. In God, whose word I praise—in the Lord, whose word I praise—in God I trust; I will not be afraid. What can man do to me?

I am under vows to you, O God; I will present my thank offerings to you. For you have delivered me from death and my feet from stumbling, that I may walk before God in the light of life.

PSALM 57

The 57th psalm is a psalm of prayer in which David once again complains about Saul and his servants—when he crawled away from them into the cave. It has the same meaning as the preceding psalm. Therefore we would make use of it also against the tyrants and their venomous counselors and slanderers, who twist God's Word against us. They have the fangs and tongue for such work, which are—as

David says—spears, arrows, and sharp swords. But thanks be to God, who does not desert us, but hurls them into the pit that they have prepared for us. Their plots finally come down on their own heads.

PSALM 57

For the director of music. To the tune of "Do Not Destroy." Of David. A miktam. When he had fled from Saul into the cave.

Have mercy on me, O God, have mercy on me, for in you my soul takes refuge. I will take refuge in the shadow of your wings until the disaster has passed.

I cry out to God Most High, to God, who fulfills his purpose for me. He sends from heaven and saves me, rebuking those who hotly pursue me; God sends his love and his faithfulness.

I am in the midst of lions; I lie among ravenous beasts—men whose teeth are spears and arrows, whose tongues are sharp swords.

Be exalted, O God, above the heavens; let your glory be over all the earth.

They spread a net for my feet—I was bowed down in distress. They dug a pit in my path—but they have fallen into it themselves.

My heart is steadfast, O God, my heart is steadfast; I will sing and make music. Awake, my soul! Awake, harp and lyre! I will awaken the dawn.

I will praise you, O Lord, among the nations; I will sing of you among the peoples. For great is your love, reaching to the heavens; your faithfulness reaches to the skies.

Be exalted, O God, above the heavens; let your glory be over all the earth.

PSALM 58

The 58th psalm is a psalm of comfort against the stiff-necked teachers who stubbornly carry through with their error, stop up their ears, and never let themselves be corrected, but rather threaten to devour the godly. The psalmist comforts himself, using five comparisons, that they will not carry out their intentions—yes, they will not accomplish half of them: (1) There comes at times a great flood with a terrible roar, as if it would carry away everything, but it flows away and does nothing. (2) A crossbow may be a severe threat, but when arrow, string, and bow are broken, it does nothing. (3) A slug stretches out its antennae, but before it moves, it is dried up or melted away. (4) A stillborn child enlarges the mother's womb, as if it will come as a baby, but dies before it sees the light. (5) A thornbush may stick out with many spikes and threaten with pricks and scratches, but before it becomes fully developed and hard, a raging hatchet descends on it and summons the thorns into the oven to become ashes. Though all of these intended to be great and proceed with success, nevertheless nothing shall come from them.

PSALM 58

For the director of music. To the tune of "Do Not Destroy." Of David. A miktam.

Do you rulers indeed speak justly? Do you judge uprightly among men? No, in your heart you devise injustice, and your hands mete out violence on the earth. Even from birth the wicked go astray; from the womb they are wayward and speak lies. Their venom is like the venom of a snake, like that of a cobra that has stopped its ears, that will not heed the tune of the charmer, however skillful the enchanter may be.

Break the teeth in their mouths, O God; tear out, O Lord, the fangs of the lions! Let them vanish like water that flows away; when they draw the bow, let their arrows be blunted. Like a slug melting away as it moves along, like a stillborn child, may they not see the sun.

Before your pots can feel the heat of the thorns—whether they be green or dry—the wicked will be swept away. The righteous will be glad when they are avenged, when they bathe their feet in the blood of the wicked. Then men will say, "Surely the righteous still are rewarded; surely there is a God who judges the earth."

PSALM 59

The 59th psalm is a psalm of prayer and can very well be spoken in the person of Christ, who lamented over those who by their teachings stood arrayed against him, to condemn and disavow him. Thereby they have their reward: they come into the city at evening like hungry dogs and yet find nothing. The psalm however can also be understood from the history of David against his "Saulites," who also are finally without a kingdom and wander around like hungry dogs until they are totally destroyed. For Saul's family never again came to the kingship, although they strived for it with eagerness and effort.

PSALM 59

For the director of music. To the tune of "Do Not Destory." Of David. A miktam. *When Saul had sent men to watch David's house in order to kill him.*

Deliver me from my enemies, O God; protect me from those who rise up against me. Deliver me from evildoers and save me from bloodthirsty men.

See how they lie in wait for me! Fierce men conspire against me for no offense or sin of mine, O Lord. I have done no wrong, yet they are ready to attack me. Arise to help me; look on my plight! O Lord God Almighty, the God of Israel, rouse yourself to punish all the nations; show no mercy to wicked traitors.

They return at evening, snarling like dogs, and prowl about the city. See what they spew from their mouths—they spew out swords from their lips, and they say, "Who can hear us?" But you, O Lord, laugh at them; you scoff at all those nations.

O my Strength, I watch for you; you, O God, are my fortress, my loving God.

God will go before me and will let me gloat over those who slander me. But do not kill them, O Lord our shield, or my people will forget. In your might make them wander about, and bring them down. For the sins of their mouths, for the words of their lips, let them be caught in their pride. For the curses and lies they utter, consume them in wrath, consume them till they are no more. Then it will be known to the ends of the earth that God rules over Jacob.

They return at evening, snarling like dogs, and prowl about the city. They wander about for food and howl if not satisfied. But I will sing of your strength, in the morning I will sing of your love; for you are my fortress, my refuge in times of trouble.

O my Strength, I sing praise to you; you, O God, are my fortress, my loving God.

PSALM 60

The 60th psalm is a psalm of thanks in which David thanks God that he has given him an excellent kingdom in which God's Word was taught and there was good, orderly government, which truly is a precious jewel. Before David, in the time of Saul, the government was disunited and chaotic, as the first three verses declare. The Philistines plagued them sorely, so that they did not take much care even for the ark of God (1 Chronicles 13). Also evil things prospered, along with much unrighteousness. So it will always be where God is not at home. David's example also points out well that Saul had evil rogues in place in his court.

Yet (he says), God kept a banner, a sign, in place for his people, so that they might rise up and praise him. Through it they could be sure and secure in his grace. This sign was the tent of Moses and the ark of the covenant with the seat of grace, which ark God also brought out of the land of the Philistines with great wonders. Before the ark they prayed and called on God and were accordingly delivered from their distress.

Thereafter, David lists his land and people, beginning with the holy sanctuary and God's Word, then Shechem, Succoth, Gilead, Manasseh, Ephraim, Judah, Moab, Edom, Philistia. Finally, he gives a confession concerning these things: To have a fortified city, that is, good peaceful government; to have victory over Edom, that is, to prevail over people and land and in the middle of battle; these are not human accomplishments but gifts from God. Why he names no more lands or tribes than the nine he names belongs in a commentary rather than this summary.

We also can say this psalm in praise of God, that he has extended his church into the wide world and into many parishes and seminaries, where each may have the Word of God and all have their various gifts.

PSALM 60

For the director of music. To the tune of "The Lily of the Covenant." A miktam of David. For teaching. When he fought Aram Naharaim and Aram Zobah, and when Joab returned and struck down twelve thousand Edomites in the Valley of Salt.

You have rejected us, O God, and burst forth upon us; you have been angry—now restore us! You have shaken the land and torn it open; mend its fractures, for it is quaking. You have shown your people desperate times; you have given us wine that makes us stagger.

But for those who fear you, you have raised a banner to be unfurled against the bow. Save us and help us with your right hand, that those you love may be delivered.

God has spoken from his sanctuary: "In triumph I will parcel out Shechem and measure off the Valley of Succoth. Gilead is mine, and Manasseh is mine; Ephraim is my helmet, Judah my scepter. Moab is my washbasin, upon Edom I toss my sandal; over Philistia I shout in triumph."

Who will bring me to the fortified city? Who will lead me to Edom? Is it not you, O God, you who have rejected us and no longer go out with our armies? Give us aid against the enemy, for the help of man is worthless. With God we will gain the victory, and he will trample down our enemies.

PSALM 61

The 61st psalm is a psalm of prayer against the enemy on behalf of the king and those in authority, that they fear God, rule long and well, and that government not be destroyed by enemy and war. For, as Solomon said (cf. Prov. 28:2): Because of the land's sin, many princes perish. But where there are many rulers, it seldom fails that what one constructs, another breaks up. As the saying goes, "New king, new law." And this continuous changing of the government is always dangerous and harmful, but it is well for the land where an old, good system of government long continues.

PSALM 61

For the director of music. With stringed instruments. Of David.

Hear my cry, O God; listen to my prayer.

From the ends of the earth I call to you, I call as my heart grows faint; lead me to the rock that is higher than I. For you have been my refuge, a strong tower against the foe.

I long to dwell in your tent forever and take refuge in the shelter of your wings. For you have heard my vows, O God; you have given me the heritage of those who fear your name.

Increase the days of the king's life, his years for many generations. May he be enthroned in God's presence forever; appoint your love and faithfulness to protect him.

Then will I ever sing praise to your name and fulfill my vows day after day.

PSALM 62

The 62nd psalm is a psalm of instruction concerning the false confidence in human powers and the true confidence in God. There are many who, having the favor of a prince or a noble or the good will of the rich and powerful, think that they need nothing more, and then do much harm. Particularly, where they see a tottering wall, that is, when they notice that someone is not well looked upon in the palace or else is in need and is persecuted by another so that he cannot defend himself, then they all become knights, and they thoroughly flatter and play up to the great nobles. They do not see how entirely vain is such trust in princes and also do not believe, until it happens, how thoroughly it shall collapse. Therefore it is said. Trust God and do wrong to no one who stands before God or men.

PSALM 62

For the director of music. For Jeduthun. A psalm of David.

My soul finds rest in God alone; my salvation comes from him. He alone is my rock and my salvation; he is my fortress, I will never be shaken.

How long will you assault a man? Would all of you throw him down—this leaning wall, this tottering fence? They fully intend to topple him from his lofty place; they take delight in lies. With their mouths they bless, but in their hearts they curse.

Find rest, O my soul, in God alone; my hope comes from him. He alone is my rock and my salvation; he is my fortress, I will not be shaken. My salvation and my honor depend on God; he is my mighty rock, my refuge. Trust in him at all times, O people; pour out your hearts to him, for God is our refuge.

Lowborn men are but a breath, the highborn are but a lie; if weighed on a balance, they are nothing; together they are only a breath. Do not trust in extortion or take pride in stolen goods; though your riches increase, do not set your heart on them.

One thing God has spoken, two things have I heard: that you, O God, are strong, and that you, O Lord, are loving. Surely you will reward each person according to what he has done.

PSALM 63

The 63rd psalm is a psalm of prayer in which David, when he had to flee into the wilderness from Saul, desired to be in the holy place and hear God's Word. He laments over the "Saulites," who seek his life so that he cannot come there and thus is deprived of the Word of God. But he meditates, nevertheless, on the promise and

God's choice of him to be king, and he comforts himself with these in the meantime.

Now however this is a psalm people can pray, who hold onto God's Word under the tyrants and yet are deprived of that Word. They consider themselves still as God's children and heirs, since they have faith and love in his Word, until their "Saul" finds his end.

PSALM 63

A psalm of David. When he was in the Desert of Judah.

O God, you are my God, earnestly I seek you; my soul thirsts for you, my body longs for you, in a dry and weary land where there is no water.

I have seen you in the sanctuary and beheld your power and your glory. Because your love is better than life, my lips will glorify you. I will praise you as long as I live, and in your name I will lift up my hands. My soul will be satisfied as with the richest of foods; with singing lips my mouth will praise you.

On my bed I remember you; I think of you through the watches of the night. Because you are my help, I sing in the shadow of your wings. My soul clings to you; your right hand upholds me.

They who seek my life will be destroyed; they will go down to the depths of the earth. They will be given over to the sword and become food for jackals. But the king will rejoice in God; all who swear by God's name will praise him, while the mouths of liars will be silenced.

PSALM 64

The 64th psalm is a psalm of prayer in which David prays against his betrayers and slanderers who made their case with poisonous words and evil malignity in the worst way—as Absalom, Ahithophel, and the like, and Doeg before, in the court of Saul. But he has this comfort, that their words would come down on themselves, and their tongues would bring down not David but themselves—as happened to Absalom, Ahithophel, and Doeg.

In like manner, we also pray against our betrayers among the courts of the princes, bishops, and kings, who today undertake various malignities, machinations, and tricks. As has already often been seen however, these tricks come down on themselves, so that people will say, "God has repaid them."

PSALM 64

For the director of music. A psalm of David.

Hear me, O God, as I voice my complaint; protect my life from the threat of the enemy. Hide me from the conspiracy of the wicked, from that noisy crowd of evildoers.

They sharpen their tongues like swords and aim their words like deadly arrows. They shoot from ambush at the innocent man; they shoot at him suddenly, without fear.

They encourage each other in evil plans, they talk about hiding their snares; they say, "Who will see them?" They plot injustice and say, "We have devised a perfect plan!" Surely the mind and heart of man are cunning.

But God will shoot them with arrows; suddenly they will be struck down. He will turn their own tongues against them and bring them to ruin; all who see them will shake their heads in scorn.

All mankind will fear; they will proclaim the works of God and ponder what he has done. Let the righteous rejoice in the Lord and take refuge in him; let all the upright in heart praise him!

PSALM 65

The 65th psalm is a psalm of thanks in which he praises God that he gives his Word and worship, and temporal peace as well. He regulates the fury of the enemy and the wars in the land, which break out and storm like the sea, and blesses the field, so that everything turns out well, produces well, grows well. Oh, how rare this praise is among the rabble, who abuse the Word of peace and prosperous times and live a totally destructive life, as Sodom and Gomorrah did. It will go as well with them at the end as with Sodom and Gomorrah.

PSALM 65

For the director of music. A psalm of David. A song.

Praise awaits you, O God, in Zion; to you our vows will be fulfilled. O you who hear prayer, to you all men will come. When we were overwhelmed by sins, you forgave our transgressions. Blessed are those you choose and bring near to live in your courts! We are filled with the good things of your house, of your holy temple.

You answer us with awesome deeds of righteousness, O God our Savior, the hope of all the ends of the earth and of the farthest seas, who formed the mountains by your power, having armed yourself with strength, who stilled the roaring of the seas, the roaring of their waves, and the turmoil of the nations. Those living far away fear your wonders; where morning dawns and evening fades you call forth songs of joy.

You care for the land and water it; you enrich it abundantly. The streams of God are filled with water to provide the people with grain, for so you have ordained it. You drench its furrows and level its ridges; you soften it with showers and bless its crops. You crown the year with your bounty, and your carts overflow with abundance. The grasslands of the desert overflow; the hills are clothed with gladness. The meadows are covered with flocks and the valleys are mantled with grain; they shout for joy and sing.

PSALM 66

The 66th psalm is a psalm of thanks for the general blessing that God often delivers and protects his people out of the hand of the enemies, as he did at the Red Sea. The histories in the books of the Judges and Kings are full of these deliverances, which he also does daily for us, delivering and keeping his own in the true faith against devil, spirits, and sins.

PSALM 66

For the director of music. A song. A psalm.

Shout with joy to God, all the earth! Sing the glory of his name; make his praise glorious! Say to God, ''How awesome are your deeds! So great is your power that your enemies cringe before you. All the earth bows down to you; they sing praise to you, they sing praise to your name.''

Come and see what God has done, how awesome his works in man's behalf! He turned the sea into dry land, they passed through the waters on foot—come, let us rejoice in him. He rules forever by his power, his eyes watch the nations—let not the rebellious rise up against him.

Praise our God, O peoples, let the sound of his praise be heard; he has preserved our lives and kept our feet from slipping. For you, O God, tested us; you refined us like silver. You brought us into prison and laid burdens on our backs. You let men ride over our heads; we went through fire and water, but you brought us to a place of abundance.

I will come to your temple with burnt offerings and fulfill my vows to you—vows my lips promised and my mouth spoke when I was in trouble. I will sacrifice fat animals to you and an offering of rams; I will offer bulls and goats.

Come and listen, all you who fear God; let me tell you what he has done for me. I cried out to him with my mouth; his praise was on my tongue. If I had cherished sin in my heart, the Lord would not have listened; but God has surely listened and heard my voice in prayer. Praise be to God, who has not rejected my prayer or withheld his love from me!

PSALM 67

The 67th psalm is a prophecy of Christ, that he shall be king the whole world over and rule the people rightly, that is, rule them with the Gospel, that they may be freed from sin to live for him in righteousness and thank him with joy. As we have often stated, this is the new and proper worship of God. For he does not say that the Gentiles shall circumcise themselves and run to Jerusalem, but rather that they will remain Gentiles and nevertheless give thanks to God, be joyful, and fear him, that is, worship him.

PSALM 67

For the director of music. With stringed instruments. A psalm. A song.

May God be gracious to us and bless us and make his face shine upon us, that your ways may be known on earth, your salvation among all nations.

May the peoples praise you, O God; may all the peoples praise you. May the nations be glad and sing for joy, for you rule the peoples justly and guide the nations of the earth. May the peoples praise you, O God; may all the peoples praise you.

Then the land will yield its harvest, and God, our God, will bless us. God will bless us, and all the ends of the earth will fear him.

PSALM 68

The 68th psalm is a beautiful and powerful prophecy of Christ, that he shall rise, ascend to heaven, give his Spirit, send his apostles, let the Gospel be preached, rescue poor sinners from death, comfort the sorrowful, destroy the Jewish kingdom and priesthood and scatter them, and establish a new kingdom in which he will daily be praised and preached, and not the law of Moses. The psalm calls the apostles kings and lords of armies and leaders in battle since, with the Gospel, they do battle against death, sin, and the devil, against the wisdom and holiness of the world. Likewise, it calls them high fruitful mountains, God's heirs, and God's chariots with many hosts. Again, it also calls them singers and choruses among the maidens, dancers, and singers—because they joyfully praise, glorify, and thank God. Thus he sings his song of joy over the holy kingdom of grace and life. He prays at the end that God keep his kingdom, bless it, and establish it to eternity. He is so completely and joyfully stirred in spirit that he has written this beautiful and rich psalm.

PSALM 68

For the director of music. Of David. A psalm. A song.

May God arise, may his enemies be scattered; may his foes flee before him. As smoke is blown away by the wind, may you blow them away; as wax melts before the fire, may the wicked perish before God. But may the righteous be glad and rejoice before God; may they be happy and joyful.

Sing to God, sing praise to his name, extol him who rides on the clouds—his name is the Lord—and rejoice before him. A father to the fatherless, a defender of widows, is God in his holy dwelling. God sets the lonely in families, he leads forth the prisoners with singing; but the rebellious live in a sun-scorched land.

When you went out before your people, O God, when you marched through the wasteland, the earth shook, the heavens poured down rain, before God, the One of Sinai, before God, the God of Israel. You gave abundant showers, O God; you refreshed your weary inheritance. Your people settled in it, and from your bounty, O God, you provided for the poor.

The Lord announced the word, and great was the company of those who proclaimed it: "Kings and armies flee in haste; in the camps men divide the plunder. Even while you sleep among the campfires, the wings of my dove are sheathed with silver, its feathers with shining gold." When the Almighty scattered the kings in the land, it was like snow fallen on Zalmon.

The mountains of Bashan are majestic mountains; rugged are the mountains of Bashan. Why gaze in envy, O rugged mountains, at the mountain where God chooses to reign, where the Lord himself will dwell forever? The chariots of God are tens of thousands and thousands of thousands; the Lord has come from Sinai into his sanctuary. When you ascended on high, you led captives in your train;

you received gifts from men, even from the rebellious—that you, O Lord God, might dwell there.

Praise be to the Lord, to God our Savior, who daily bears our burdens. Our God is a God who saves; from the Sovereign Lord comes escape from death.

Surely God will crush the heads of his enemies, the hairy crowns of those who go on in their sins. The Lord says, ''I will bring them from Bashan; I will bring them from the depths of the sea, that you may plunge your feet in the blood of your foes, while the tongues of your dogs have their share.''

Your procession has come into view, O God, the procession of my God and King into the sanctuary. In front are the singers, after them the musicians; with them are the maidens playing tambourines. Praise God in the great congregation; praise the Lord in the assembly of Israel. There is the little tribe of Benjamin, leading them, there the great throng of Judah's princes, and there the princes of Zebulun and of Naphtali.

Summon your power, O God; show us your strength, O God, as you have done before. Because of your temple at Jerusalem kings will bring you gifts. Rebuke the beast among the reeds, the herd of bulls among the calves of the nations. Humbled, may it bring bars of silver. Scatter the nations who delight in war. Envoys will come from Egypt; Cush will submit herself to God.

Sing to God, O kingdoms of the earth, sing praise to the Lord, to him who rides the ancient skies above, who thunders with mighty voice. Proclaim the power of God, whose majesty is over Israel, whose power is in the skies. You are awesome, O God, in your sanctuary; the God of Israel gives power and strength to his people.

Praise be to God!

PSALM 69

The 69th psalm is a psalm of prayer in the person of Christ as he spoke on the cross in his suffering. He confesses in our place and laments for his crucifiers and slanderers who, in his great thirst, gave him gall and vinegar to drink. (So clearly and openly he speaks of his suffering to come.) Then he prophesies of the horrible delusion, hardness of heart, and ultimate defeat of the Jews, which has all come about, as we can still see and sorrow over.

Finally, he announces also the new worship. He says: "I will praise God and glorify him with thanksgiving." This worship shall put an end to the old, for it pleases God better than all bulls and the best offerings one can provide, as the psalm here says.

PSALM 69

For the director of music. To the tune of "Lilies." Of David.

Save me, O God, for the waters have come up to my neck. I sink in the miry depths, where there is no foothold. I have come into the deep waters; the floods engulf me. I am worn out calling for help; my throat is parched. My eyes fail, looking for my God. Those who hate me without reason outnumber the hairs of my head; many are my enemies without cause, those who seek to destroy me. I am forced to restore what I did not steal.

You know my folly, O God; my guilt is not hidden from you.

May those who hope in you not be disgraced because of me, O Lord, the Lord Almighty; may those who seek you not be put to shame because of me, O God of Israel. For I endure scorn for your sake, and shame covers my face. I am a stranger to my brothers, an alien to my own mother's sons; for zeal for your house consumes me, and the insults of those who insult you fall on me. When I weep and fast, I must endure scorn; when I put on sackcloth, people make sport of me. Those who sit at the gate mock me, and I am the song of the drunkards.

But I pray to you, O Lord, in the time of your favor; in your great love, O God, answer me with your sure salvation. Rescue me from the mire, do not let me sink; deliver me from those who hate me, from the deep waters. Do not let the floodwaters engulf me or the depths swallow me up or the pit close its mouth over me. Answer me, O Lord, out of the goodness of your love; in your great mercy turn to me. Do not hide your face from your servant; answer me quickly, for I am in trouble. Come near and rescue me; redeem me because of my foes.

You know how I am scorned, disgraced and shamed; all my enemies are before you. Scorn has broken my heart and has left me helpless; I looked for sympathy, but there was none, for comforters, but I found none. They put gall in my food and gave me vinegar for my thirst.

May the table set before them become a snare; may it become retribution and a trap. May their eyes be darkened so they cannot see, and their backs be bent forever. Pour out your wrath on them; let your fierce anger overtake them. May their place be deserted; let there be no one to dwell in their tents. For they persecute those you wound and talk about the pain of those you hurt. Charge them with crime upon crime; do not let them share in your salvation. May they be blotted out of the book of life and not be listed with the righteous.

I am in pain and distress; may your salvation, O God, protect me.

I will praise God's name in song and glorify him with thanksgiving. This will please the Lord more than an ox, more than a bull with its horns and hoofs. The poor will see and be glad—you who seek God, may your hearts live! The Lord hears the needy and does not despise his captive people.

Let heaven and earth praise him, the seas and all that move in them, for God will save Zion and rebuild the cities of Judah. Then people will settle there and possess it; the children of his servants will inherit it, and those who love his name will dwell there.

PSALM 70

The 70th psalm is a psalm of prayer against the persecutors and enemies of the godly. With fist and deed, with counsel and wishes in the heart, with word and cry—that is, with earnestness and all diligence—they seek to take the life of the godly because of God's Word.

PSALM 70

For the director of music. Of David. A petition.

Hasten, O God, to save me; O Lord, come quickly to help me. May those who seek my life be put to shame and confusion; may all who desire my ruin be turned back in disgrace. May those who say to me, "Aha! Aha!" turn back because of their shame. But may all who seek you rejoice and be glad in you; may those who love your salvation always say, "Let God be exalted!"

Yet I am poor and needy; come quickly to me, O God. You are my help and my deliverer; O Lord, do not delay.

PSALM 71

The 71st psalm is (by my understanding) a psalm of prayer spoken from beginning to end in the person of all Christendom against all enemies and affliction. It prays especially concerning the time of old age, when one becomes feeble and grey. That is, it prays for the last Christians, for whom the times will be dangerous, and when faith—together with the Gospel—will be cast down. In the same way, Daniel also proclaimed that the truth would be cast down and unrighteousness shall conquer. Therefore the psalmist praises God's righteousness alone, which he has learned from God since his youth, or since the beginning.

May this be a comforting prophecy for us, that God's Word shall return before the end of the world. With this Word God will call us from the depths of the earth and mightily comfort us. From this basis comes also the general statements concerning Christ: that Elijah and Enoch shall come, the lies of the antichrist shall be exposed, and all shall again be set right.

PSALM 71

In you, O Lord, I have taken refuge; let me never be put to shame. Rescue me and deliver me in your righteousness; turn your ear to me and save me. Be my rock of refuge, to which I can always go; give the command to save me, for you are my rock and my fortress. Deliver me, O my God, from the hand of the wicked, from the grasp of evil and cruel men.

For you have been my hope, O Sovereign Lord, my confidence since my youth. From birth I have relied on you; you brought me forth from my mother's womb. I will ever praise you. I have become like a portent to many, but you are my strong refuge. My mouth is filled with your praise, declaring your splendor all day long.

Do not cast me away when I am old; do not forsake me when my strength is gone. For my enemies speak against me; those who wait to kill me conspire together. They say, "God has forsaken him; pursue him and seize him, for no one will rescue him." Be not far from me, O God; come quickly, O my God, to help me. May my accusers perish in shame; may those who want to harm me be covered with scorn and disgrace.

But as for me, I will always have hope; I will praise you more and more. My mouth will tell of your righteousness, of your salvation all day long, though I know not its measure. I will come and proclaim your mighty acts, O Sovereign Lord; I will proclaim your righteousness, yours alone. Since my youth, O God, you have taught me, and to this day I declare your marvelous deeds. Even when I am old and gray, do not forsake me, O God, till I declare your power to the next generation, your might to all who are to come.

Your righteousness reaches to the skies, O God, you who have done great things. Who, O God, is like you? Though you have made me see troubles, many and bitter, you will restore my life again; from the depths of the earth you will again bring me up. You will increase my honor and comfort me once again.

I will praise you with the harp for your faithfulness, O my God; I will sing praise to you with the lyre, O Holy One of Israel. My lips will shout for joy when I sing praise to you—I, whom you have redeemed. My tongue will tell of your righteous acts all day long, for those who wanted to harm me have been put to shame and confusion.

PSALM 72

The 72nd psalm is an exceedingly magnificent and beautiful prophecy of Christ and his rule in the whole world. In this kingdom, neither sin nor the evil conscience shall flower and reign (as under the law) but only righteousness, freedom, and joy of conscience. However, this is not without cross. On account of the cross, their blood shall be shed, which blood however is counted as very precious to God. And the psalm also announces the new worship, which is to call on God and to thank him. He tells us to pray to God daily and daily to praise him. This is our daily offering among all the Gentiles. Here we hear nothing of circumcision, nor yet that the kings and Gentiles should receive the law of Moses, but rather that they remain kings and Gentiles and receive this king as truly God by nature, call on him, and glorify him. For to call on God in distress and thank him for his help is the worship that alone pleases him, who is alone our helper in need and our Savior. Without him, all else is no help at all.

PSALM 72

Of Solomon.

Endow the king with your justice, O God, the royal son with your righteousness. He will judge your people in righteousness, your afflicted ones with justice. The mountains will bring prosperity to the people, the hills the fruit of righteousness. He will defend the afflicted among the people and save the children of the needy; he will crush the oppressor.

He will endure as long as the sun, as long as the moon, through all generations. He will be like rain falling on a mown field, like showers watering the earth. In his days the righteous will flourish; prosperity will abound till the moon is no more.

He will rule from sea to sea and from the River to the ends of the earth. The desert tribes will bow before him and his enemies will lick the dust. The kings of Tarshish and of distant shores will bring tribute to him; the kings of Sheba and Seba will present him gifts. All kings will bow down to him and all nations will serve him.

For he will deliver the needy who cry out, the afflicted who have no one to help. He will take pity on the weak and the needy and save the needy from death. He will rescue them from oppression and violence, for precious is their blood in his sight.

Long may he live! May gold from Sheba be given him. May people ever pray for him and bless him all day long. Let grain abound throughout the land; on the tops of the hills may it sway. Let its fruit flourish like Lebanon; let it thrive like the grass of the field. May his name endure forever; may it continue as long as the sun.

All nations will be blessed through him, and they will call him blessed.

Praise be to the Lord God, the God of Israel, who alone does marvelous deeds. Praise be to his glorious name forever; may the whole earth be filled with his glory. Amen and Amen.

PSALM 73

The 73rd psalm is a psalm of instruction against the great vexation that the godless are rich and everything goes well for them. They ridicule the poor and afflicted saints as if God neither knew nor regarded them. They consider only themselves and their holy works and what they taught and said as precious, heavenly, and godly wisdom and holiness. This causes much pain, so that the psalmist says, "I was senseless before you," that is, I was called a godless heretic and despiser of God. Then, he says, "Stop! Go into the sanctuary and hear what God's Word says of them. Look at the former examples in the histories, and you will find that they all at once come to nothing, for there is no ground or foundation under them, but only slippery footing."

PSALM 73

A psalm of Asaph.

Surely God is good to Israel, to those who are pure in heart.

But as for me, my feet had almost slipped; I had nearly lost my foothold. For I envied the arrogant when I saw the prosperity of the wicked.

They have no struggles; their bodies are healthy and strong. They are free from the burdens common to man; they are not plagued by human ills. Therefore pride is their necklace; they clothe themselves with violence. From their callous hearts comes iniquity; the evil conceits of their minds know no limits. They scoff, and speak with malice; in their arrogance they threaten oppression. Their mouths lay claim to heaven, and their tongues take possession of the earth. Therefore their people turn to them and drink up waters in abundance. They say, "How can God know? Does the Most High have knowledge?"

This is what the wicked are like—always carefree, they increase in wealth.

Surely in vain have I kept my heart pure; in vain have I washed my hands in innocence. All day long I have been plagued; I have been punished every morning.

If I had said, "I will speak thus," I would have betrayed your children. When I tried to understand all this, it was oppressive to me till I entered the sanctuary of God; then I understood their final destiny.

Surely you place them on slippery ground; you cast them down to ruin. How suddenly are they destroyed, completely swept away by terrors! As a dream when one awakes, so when you arise, O Lord, you will despise them as fantasies.

When my heart was grieved and my spirit embittered, I was senseless and ignorant; I was a brute beast before you.

Yet I am always with you; you hold me by my right hand. You guide me with your counsel, and afterward you will take me into glory. Whom have I in heaven but you? And earth has nothing I desire besides you. My flesh and my heart may fail, but God is the strength of my heart and my portion forever.

Those who are far from you will perish; you destroy all who are unfaithful to you. But as for me, it is good to be near God. I have made the Sovereign Lord my refuge; I will tell of all your deeds.

PSALM 74

The 74th psalm is a psalm of prayer against the enemies who had laid waste Jerusalem, the temple, and all the schools of God in the land, together with the cities. Moreover, they slandered God, saying he could not help his people. It appears however as if it were a prayer against the destruction still to come, that is, of the Babylonians and thereafter by Antiochus Epiphanes. For only in these two instances were the temple in Jerusalem and the land destroyed. Accordingly, we pray this psalm against those who devastate Christendom, tear up God's Word, Sacrament, and all of God's ordinances, and thus clearly preach abomination and slander, and who continue everywhere.

PSALM 74

A maskil *of Asaph.*

Why have you rejected us forever, O God? Why does your anger smolder against the sheep of your pasture? Remember the people you purchased of old, the tribe of your inheritance, whom you redeemed—Mount Zion, where you dwelt. Turn your steps toward these everlasting ruins, all this destruction the enemy has brought on the sanctuary.

Your foes roared in the place where you met with us; they set up their standards as signs. They behaved like men wielding axes to cut through a thicket of trees. They smashed all the carved paneling with their axes and hatchets. They burned your sanctuary to the ground; they defiled the dwelling place of your Name. They said in their hearts, "We will crush them completely!" They burned every place where God was worshiped in the land. We are given no miraculous signs; no prophets are left, and none of us knows how long this will be.

How long will the enemy mock you, O God? Will the foe revile your name forever? Why do you hold back your hand, your right hand? Take it from the folds of your garment and destroy them!

But you, O God, are my king from of old; you bring salvation upon the earth. It was you who split open the sea by your power; you broke the heads of the monster in the waters. It was you who crushed the heads of Leviathan and gave him as food to the creatures of the desert. It was you who opened up springs and streams; you dried up the ever flowing rivers. The day is yours, and yours also the night; you established the sun and moon. It was you who set all the boundaries of the earth; you made both summer and winter.

Remember how the enemy has mocked you, O Lord, how foolish people have reviled your name. Do not hand over the life of your dove to wild beasts; do not forget the lives of your afflicted people forever. Have regard for your covenant, because haunts of violence fill the dark places of the land. Do not let the oppressed retreat in disgrace; may the poor and needy praise your name.

Rise up, O God, and defend your cause; remember how fools mock you all day long. Do not ignore the clamor of your adversaries, the uproar of your enemies, which rises continually.

PSALM 75

The 75th psalm is a psalm of comfort against the stiff-necked, proud, godless teachers who are self-secure and presume on their office, as if they need fear nothing, neither threat nor punishment. As Psalm 73 above has written: Who shall be our teacher? We are the teachers! We sit in the office, we have the power, and all must obey us or be excommunicated as heretics. So also today our secure princes and the rebellious spirits sit as spiritual and worldly tyrants, thinking that God himself can neither see nor overthrow them.

But this psalm says otherwise. It gives us the comfort that we should look forward to the judgment, when they will be judged and pass away. The earth will shake and tremble with all its inhabitants; nevertheless God will preserve the pillars, that is, the godly who bear and preserve this world, as St. Paul (1 Tim. 3:15) calls the church a foundation and a pillar of truth. Thus, God preserved Lot when he overthrew Sodom and preserved the believing Jews with the apostles when he destroyed the Jewish nation. For he well knows how to deliver his own when he destroys a land.

PSALM 75

For the director of music. To the tune of "Do Not Destroy." A psalm of Asaph. A song.

We give thanks to you, O God, we give thanks, for your Name is near; men tell of your wonderful deeds.

You say, "I choose the appointed time; it is I who judge uprightly. When the earth and all its people quake, it is I who hold its pillars firm. To the arrogant I say, 'Boast no more,' and to the wicked, 'Do not lift up your horns. Do not lift your horns against heaven; do not speak with outstretched neck.' "

No one from the east or the west or from the desert can exalt a man. But it is God who judges: He brings one down, he exalts another. In the hand of the Lord is a cup full of foaming wine mixed with spices; he pours it out, and all the wicked of the earth drink it down to its very dregs.

As for me, I will declare this forever; I will sing praise to the God of Jacob. I will cut off the horns of all the wicked, but the horns of the righteous will be lifted up.

PSALM 76

The 76th psalm is a psalm of thanks, similar to the 46th psalm. For it gives thanks that God has his dwelling, Word, and worship in Jerusalem and that he magnificently protects his people against the kings and the rage of warriors such as Sennacherib, by which they would be devoured. For he knew how to take courage away from princes and make them discouraged.

In the same way he fights against our enemies. Be they as strong and as evil as they may, it is hard for them to defend themselves against him who takes away at once their heart and courage. Even the devil flees when his courage fails him. What then can flesh and blood do? Such a warrior-God must be praised, who deals thus with the noise of kings. He can save his own, without a sword, by fright and fear alone.

PSALM 76

For the director of music. With stringed instruments. A psalm of Asaph. A song.

In Judah God is known; his name is great in Israel. His tent is in Salem, his dwelling place in Zion. There he broke the flashing arrows, the shields and the swords, the weapons of war.

You are resplendent with light, more majestic than mountains rich with game. Valiant men lie plundered, they sleep their last sleep; not one of the warriors can lift his hands. At your rebuke, O God of Jacob, both horse and chariot lie still. You alone are to be feared. Who can stand before you when you are angry? From heaven you pronounced judgment, and the land feared and was quiet—when you, O God, rose up to judge, to save all the afflicted of the land. Surely your wrath against men brings you praise, and the survivors of your wrath are restrained.

Make vows to the Lord your God and fulfill them; let all the neighboring lands bring gifts to the One to be feared. He breaks the spirit of rulers; he is feared by the kings of the earth.

PSALM 77

The 77th psalm is a psalm of instruction. The psalmist uses himself as an example of how to find comfort when affliction comes and the conscience is troubled, as if God is angry with it. He says that he was so troubled that he could not have any sleep or even speak. But this comfort follows, that he can fight off the thoughts with which he futilely suffered, and that he can grasp instead the thought of the mighty works of God in the histories of old. Here we find that God's work was to help the miserable, the troubled, and the abandoned, and to throw down the self-secure, proud scoffer, for example, when he delivered the children of Israel from Egypt.

For this reason his paths are called "hidden." He is there to help when we think that we are totally abandoned. We should learn this well. God intends by this psalm to show us and teach us his manner of helping, namely that we are never abandoned by God when things go ill. Instead we should wait upon his help at that time with the greatest confidence and not believe our thoughts.

PSALM 77

For the director of music. For Jeduthun. Of Asaph. A psalm.

I cried out to God for help; I cried out to God to hear me. When I was in distress, I sought the Lord; at night I stretched out untiring hands and my soul refused to be comforted.

I remembered you, O God, and I groaned; I mused, and my spirit grew faint.

You kept my eyes from closing; I was too troubled to speak. I thought about the former days, the years of long ago; I remembered my songs in the night. My heart mused and my spirit inquired:

"Will the Lord reject forever? Will he never show his favor again? Has his unfailing love vanquished forever? Has his promise failed for all time? Has God forgotten to be merciful? Has he in anger withheld his compassion?"

Then I thought, "To this I will appeal: the years of the right hand of the Most High." I will remember the deeds of the Lord; yes, I will remember your miracles of long ago. I will meditate on all your works and consider all your mighty deeds.

Your ways, O God, are holy. What god is so great as our God? You are the God who performs miracles; you display your power among the peoples. With your mighty arm you redeemed your people, the descendants of Jacob and Joseph.

The waters saw you, O God, the waters saw you and writhed; the very depths were convulsed. The clouds poured down water, the skies resounded with thunder; your arrows flashed back and forth. Your thunder was heard in the whirlwind, your lightning lit up the world; the earth trembled and quaked. Your path led through the sea, your way through the mighty waters, though your footprints were not seen.

You led your people like a flock by the hand of Moses and Aaron.

PSALM 78

The 78th psalm is a psalm of instruction. Using the example and history of the entire people of Israel from the beginning until David, it teaches us to trust and to believe in God, and it warns us against mistrust and faithlessness. It declares the punishment that follows faithlessness and the grace that comes with trust.

PSALM 78

A maskil *of Asaph.*

O my people, hear my teaching; listen to the words of my mouth. I will open my mouth in parables, I will utter hidden things, things from of old—what we have heard and known, what our fathers have told us. We will not hide them from their children; we will tell the next generation the praiseworthy deeds of the Lord, his power, and the wonders he has done. He decreed statutes for Jacob and established the law in Israel, which he commanded our forefathers to teach their children, so the next generation would know them, even the children yet to be born, and they in turn would tell their children. Then they would put their trust in God and would not forget his deeds but would keep his commands. They would not be like their forefathers—a stubborn and rebellious generation, whose hearts were not loyal to God, whose spirits were not faithful to him.

The men of Ephraim, though armed with bows, turned back on the day of battle; they did not keep God's covenant and refused to live by his law. They forgot what he had done, the wonders he had shown them. He did miracles in the sight of their fathers in the land of Egypt, in the region of Zoan. He divided the sea and led them through; he made the water stand firm like a wall. He guided them with the cloud by day and with light from the fire all night. He split the rocks in the desert and gave them water as abundant as the seas; he brought streams out of a rocky crag and made water flow down like rivers.

But they continued to sin against him, rebelling in the desert against the Most High. They willfully put God to the test by demanding the food they craved. They spoke against God, saying, "Can God spread a table in the desert? When he struck the rock, water gushed out, and streams flowed abundantly. But can he also give us food? Can he supply meat for his people?" When the Lord heard them, he was very angry; his fire broke out against Jacob, and his wrath rose against Israel, for they did not believe in God or trust in his deliverance. Yet he gave a command to the skies above and opened the doors of the heavens; he rained down manna for the people to eat, he gave them the grain of heaven. Men ate the bread of angels; he sent them all the food they could eat. He let loose the east wind from the heavens and led forth the south wind by his power. He rained meat down on them like dust, flying birds like sand on the seashore. He made them come down inside their camp, all around their tents. They ate till they had more than enough, for he had given them what they craved. But before they turned from the food they craved, even while it was still in their mouths, God's anger rose against them; he put to death the sturdiest among them, cutting down the young men of Israel.

In spite of all this, they kept on sinning; in spite of his wonders, they did not believe. So he ended their days in futility and their years in terror. Whenever God slew them, they would seek him; they eagerly turned to him again. They remembered that God was their Rock, that God Most High was their Redeemer. But then they would flatter him with their mouths, lying to him with their tongues; their hearts were not loyal to him, they were not faithful to his covenant. Yet he was merciful; he forgave their iniquities and did not destroy them. Time after time he restrained his anger and did not stir up his full wrath. He remembered that they were but flesh, a passing breeze that does not return.

How often they rebelled against him in the desert and grieved him in the wasteland! Again and again they put God to the test; they vexed the Holy One of Israel. They did not remember his power— the day he redeemed them from the oppressor, the day he displayed his miraculous signs in Egypt, his wonders in the region of Zoan. He turned their rivers to blood; they could not drink from their streams. He sent swarms of flies that devoured them, and frogs that devastated them. He gave their crops to the grasshopper, their produce to the locust. He destroyed their vines with hail and their sycamore-figs with sleet. He gave over their cattle to the hail, their livestock to bolts of lightning. He unleashed against them his hot anger, his wrath, indignation and hostility—a band of destroying angels. He prepared a path for his anger; he did not spare them from death but gave them over to the plague. He struck down all the firstborn of Egypt, the firstfruits of manhood in the tents of Ham. But he brought his people out like a flock; he led them like sheep through the desert. He guided them safely, so they were unafraid; but the sea engulfed their enemies. Thus he brought them to the border of his holy land, to the hill country his right hand had taken. He drove out nations before them and allotted their lands to them as an inheritance; he settled the tribes of Israel in their homes.

But they put God to the test and rebelled against the Most High; they did not keep his statutes. Like their fathers they were disloyal and faithless, as unreliable as a faulty bow. They angered him with their high places; they aroused his jealousy with their idols. When God heard them, he was very angry; he rejected Israel completely. He abandoned the tabernacle of Shiloh, the tent he had set up among men. He sent the ark of his might into captivity, his splendor into the hands of the enemy. He gave his people over to the sword; he was very angry with his inheritance. Fire consumed their young men, and their maidens had no wedding songs; their priests were put to the sword, and their widows could not weep.

Then the Lord awoke as from sleep, as a man wakes from the stupor of wine. He beat back his enemies; he put them to everlasting shame.

Then he rejected the tents of Joseph, he did not choose the tribe of Ephraim; but he chose the tribe of Judah, Mount Zion, which he loved. He built his sanctuary like the heights, like the earth that he established forever. He chose David his servant and took him from the sheep pens; from tending the sheep he brought him to be the shepherd of his people Jacob, of Israel his inheritance. And David shepherded them with integrity of heart; with skillful hands he led them.

PSALM 79

The 79th psalm is a psalm of prayer against the destruction to come, which was accomplished by the Babylonians and by Antiochus Epiphanes. It is like the 78th psalm, so the same summary applies. Isaiah 63 also prays concerning this coming destruction.

PSALM 79

A psalm of Asaph.

O God, the nations have invaded your inheritance; they have defiled your holy temple, they have reduced Jerusalem to rubble. They have given the dead bodies of your servants as food to the birds of the air, the flesh of your saints to the beasts of the earth. They have poured out blood like water all around Jerusalem, and there is no one to bury the dead. We are objects of reproach to our neighbors, of scorn and derision to those around us.

How long, O Lord? Will you be angry forever? How long will your jealousy burn like fire? Pour out your wrath on the nations that do not acknowledge you, on the kingdoms that do not call on your name; for they have devoured Jacob and destroyed his homeland. Do not hold against us the sins of the fathers; may your mercy come quickly to meet us, for we are in desperate need.

Help us, O God our Savior, for the glory of your name; deliver us and forgive our sins for your name's sake. Why should the nations say, ''Where is their God?'' Before our eyes, make known among the nations that you avenge the outpoured blood of your servants.

106

May the groans of the prisoners come before you; by the strength of your arm preserve those condemned to die.

Pay back into the laps of our neighbors seven times the reproach they have hurled at you, O Lord. Then we your people, the sheep of your pasture, will praise you forever; from generation to generation we will recount your praise.

PSALM 80

The 80th psalm is a psalm of prayer against the constant enemies, the neighboring peoples, the Philistines, Syrians, Moabites, and Edomites, who surrounded the people of Israel, pestering and attacking them. So now also we pray against our enemies and neighbors, the rebellious spirits, and the spiritual "fathers" and orders, as we have prayed in times past against the heretics of the church.

PSALM 80

For the director of music. To the tune of "The Lilies of the Covenant." Of Asaph. A psalm.

Hear us, O Shepherd of Israel, you who lead Joseph like a flock; you who sit enthroned between the cherubim, shine forth before Ephraim, Benjamin and Manasseh. Awaken your might; come and save us.

Restore us, O God; make your face shine upon us, that we may be saved.

O Lord God Almighty, how long will your anger smolder against the prayers of your people? You have fed them with the bread of tears; you have made them drink tears by the bowlful. You have made us a source of contention to our neighbors, and our enemies mock us.

Restore us, O God Almighty; make your face shine upon us, that we may be saved.

You brought a vine out of Egypt; you drove out the nations and planted it. You cleared the ground for it, and it took root and filled the land. The mountains were covered with its shade, the mighty cedars with its branches. It sent out its boughs to the Sea, its shoots as far as the River.

Why have you broken down its walls so that all who pass by pick its grapes? Boars from the forest ravage it and the creatures of the field feed on it. Return to us, O God Almighty! Look down from heaven and see! Watch over this vine, the root your right hand has planted, the son you have raised up for yourself.

Your vine is cut down, it is burned with fire; at your rebuke your people perish. Let your hand rest on the man at your right hand, the son of man you have raised up for yourself. Then we will not turn away from you; revive us, and we will call on your name.

Restore us, O Lord God Almighty; make your face shine upon us, that we may be saved.

PSALM 81

The 81st psalm is a psalm of prayer. It is a song sung and preached in the harvest season at the festival of tabernacles, calling the people back to the first commandment, that they should have only one God—he who had brought them out of the land of Egypt—and should praise and call on no other. But they did not keep this command, but instead their mouth and instruction were full of idolatry, whereas they ought to have been full of the true God and should have always spoken of him alone. This psalm teaches us to believe in Christ and cling to him alone and never commend any work as righteous before God. We also should have our mouth full of Christ, yet we also do not do this. Each one follows his own self-conceit and idol.

PSALM 81

For the director of music. According to gittith. *Of Asaph.*

Sing for joy to God our strength; shout aloud to the God of Jacob! Begin the music, strike the tambourine, play the melodious harp and lyre.

Sound the ram's horn at the New Moon, and when the moon is full, on the day of our Feast; this is a decree for Israel, an ordinance of the God of Jacob. He established it as a statute for Joseph when he went out against Egypt, where we heard a language we did not understand.

He says, "I removed the burden from their shoulders; their hands were set free from the basket. In your distress you called and I rescued you, I answered you out of a thundercloud; I tested you at the waters of Meribah.

"Hear, O my people, and I will warn you—if you would but listen to me, O Israel! You shall have no foreign god among you; you shall not bow down to an alien god. I am the Lord your God, who brought you up out of Egypt. Open wide your mouth and I will fill it.

"But my people would not listen to me; Israel would not submit to me. So I gave them over to their stubborn hearts to follow their own devices.

"If my people would but listen to me, if Israel would follow my ways, how quickly would I subdue their enemies and turn my hand against their foes! Those who hate the Lord would cringe before him, and their punishment would last forever. But you would be fed with the finest of wheat; with honey from the rock I would satisfy you."

PSALM 82

The 82nd psalm is a psalm of comfort against the tyrants who oppress those in misery. But this psalm has already had its interpretation, which has long been published.

[From Luther's commentary on Psalm 82:] After the Gospel or the ministry, there is on earth no better jewel, no greater treasure, nor richer alms, no fairer endowment, no finer posession than a ruler who makes and preserves just laws. Such men are rightly called gods. . . .

[But] worldly government will make no progress. The people are too wicked, and the lords dishonor God's name and Word continually by the shameful abuse of their godhead. Therefore he prays for another government and kingdom in which things will be better, where God's name will be honored, his Word kept, and he himself be served; that is the kingdom of Christ. . . .

For Christ practices aright the three divine virtues. . . . He advances God's Word and the preachers of it; he makes and keeps law for the poor; he protects and rescues the miserable. The service of God in Christendom is justice, peace, righteousness, life, salvation. Of this kingdom of Christ the Gospels, and the Epistles of the apostles, preach and testify. (Luther's Works, American Edition 13:54, 72)

PSALM 82

A psalm of Asaph.

God presides in the great assembly; he gives judgment among the ''gods'':

''How long will you defend the unjust and show partiality to the wicked? Defend the cause of the weak and fatherless; maintain the rights of the poor and oppressed. Rescue the weak and needy; deliver them from the hand of the wicked.

''They know nothing, they understand nothing. They walk about in darkness; all the foundations of the earth are shaken.

''I said, 'You are ''gods''; you are all sons of the Most High.' But you will die like mere men; you will fall like every other ruler.''

Rise up, O God, judge the earth, for all the nations are your inheritance.

PSALM 83

The 83rd psalm is a psalm of prayer. It is much the same as Psalm 80, which clearly spells out the names of the Gentile nations; therefore the same summary applies.

PSALM 83

A song. A psalm of Asaph.

O God, do not keep silent; be not quiet, O God, be not still. See how your enemies are astir, how your foes rear their heads. With cunning they conspire against your people; they plot against those you cherish. "Come," they say, "let us destroy them as a nation, that the name of Israel be remembered no more."

With one mind they plot together; they form an alliance against you—the tents of Edom and the Ishmaelites, of Moab and the Hagrites, Gebal, Ammon and Amalek, Philistia, with the people of Tyre. Even Assyria has joined them to lend strength to the descendants of Lot.

Do to them as you did to Midian, as you did to Sisera and Jabin at the river Kishon, who perished at Endor and became like refuse on the ground. Make their nobles like Oreb and Zeeb, all their princes like Zebah and Zalmunna, who said, "Let us take possession of the pasturelands of God."

Make them like tumbleweed, O my God, like chaff before the wind. As fire consumes the forest or a flame sets the mountains ablaze, so pursue them with your tempest and terrify them with your storm. Cover their faces with shame so that men will seek your name, O Lord.

May they ever be ashamed and dismayed; may they perish in disgrace. Let them know that you, whose name is the Lord—that you alone are the Most High over all the earth.

PSALM 84

The 84th psalm is a psalm of comfort. It praises God's Word highly over all things and exhorts us to gladly give up all good things—glory, power, joy, and whatever we desire—that we may hold onto God's Word. And if we should be like the doorkeeper, that is, the least of those in the temple, this would still be far better than to sit in all the castles of the godless. For God's Word (the psalmist says) gives victory, salvation, grace, glory, and all good things. Oh, how blessed are those who believe this and then keep it! But where are they? Even if they were slandered and despised, they would find the whole world to be theirs in abundance, prepared for them.

PSALM 84

For the director of music. According to gittith. *Of the Sons of Korah. A psalm.*

How lovely is your dwelling place, O Lord Almighty! My soul yearns, even faints, for the courts of the Lord; my heart and my flesh cry out for the living God.

Even the sparrow has found a home, and the swallow a nest for herself, where she may have her young—a place near your altar, O Lord Almighty, my King and my God. Blessed are those who dwell in your house; they are ever praising you.

Blessed are those whose strength is in you, who have set their hearts on pilgrimage. As they pass through the Valley of Baca, they make it a place of springs; the autumn rains also cover it with pools. They go from strength to strength, till each appears before God in Zion.

Hear my prayer, O Lord God Almighty; listen to me, O God of Jacob. Look upon our shield, O God; look with favor on your anointed one.

Better is one day in your courts than a thousand elsewhere; I would rather be a doorkeeper in the house of my God than dwell in the tents of the wicked. For the Lord God is a sun and shield; the Lord bestows favor and honor; no good thing does he withhold from those whose walk is blameless.

O Lord Almighty, blessed is the man who trusts in you.

PSALM 85

The 85th psalm is a psalm of prayer in which the psalmist pleads against God's wrath and seeks his grace. The wrath (in my opinion) consists in this, that they have a lack of God's Word and true preaching; also a lack of good government, peace, and godly authority; and finally a lack of fruitful times and good harvest. These afflictions hang together, one with the other. Therefore he prays that God would speak again, so that his people will not fall into folly, blaspheme in impatience, nor seek other gods; so that peace, unity, truth, and love might wash over his people and the land be fruitful; so that they can live a proper and honorable life in a God-pleasing way in peace and quietness, as St. Paul (1 Tim. 2:2) also teaches us to pray.

PSALM 85

For the director of music. Of the Sons of Korah. A psalm.

You showed favor to your land, O Lord; you restored the fortunes of Jacob. You forgave the iniquity of your people and covered all their sins. You set aside all your wrath and turned from your fierce anger.

Restore us again, O God our Savior, and put away your displeasure toward us. Will you be angry with us forever? Will you prolong your anger through all generations? Will you not revive us again, that your people may rejoice in you? Show us your unfailing love, O Lord, and grant us your salvation.

I will listen to what God the Lord will say; he promises peace to his people, his saints—but let them not return to folly. Surely his salvation is near those who fear him, that his glory may dwell in our land.

Love and faithfulness meet together; righteousness and peace kiss each other. Faithfulness springs forth from the earth, and righteousness looks down from heaven. The Lord will indeed give what is good, and our land will yield its harvest. Righteousness goes before him and prepares the way for his steps.

PSALM 86

The 86th psalm is a psalm of prayer. The title itself calls it "a prayer of David." It is easy and clear to understand. In his distress, David calls on his God against his enemies who seek to put him to death, whether that be Saul, Absalom, or whoever it may be. But notice how richly and masterfully he praises God for his goodness, faithfulness, and power, so that he may truly excite his own faith and bring warmth to his prayer. So should we do also. The sign he desires is that God would finally help him so that it would be said: God has helped him and taken his side against the rage of his enemies, who have violated God's rule.

PSALM 86

A prayer of David.

Hear, O Lord, and answer me, for I am poor and needy. Guard my life, for I am devoted to you. You are my God; save your servant who trusts in you. Have mercy on me, O Lord, for I call to you all day long. Bring joy to your servant, for to you, O Lord, I lift up my soul.

You are forgiving and good, O Lord, abounding in love to all who call to you. Hear my prayer, O Lord; listen to my cry for mercy. In the day of my trouble I will call to you, for you will answer me.

Among the gods there is none like you, O Lord; no deeds can compare with yours. All the nations you have made will come and worship before you, O Lord; they will bring glory to your name. For you are great and do marvelous deeds; you alone are God.

Teach me your way, O Lord, and I will walk in your truth; give me an undivided heart, that I may fear your name. I will praise you, O Lord my God, with all my heart; I will glorify your name forever. For great is your love toward me; you have delivered me from the depths of the grave.

The arrogant are attacking me, O God; a band of ruthless men seeks my life—men without regard for you. But you, O Lord, are a compassionate and gracious God, slow to anger, abounding in love and faithfulness. Turn to me and have mercy on me; grant your strength to your servant and save the son of your maidservant. Give me a sign of your goodness, that my enemies may see it and be put to shame, for you, O Lord, have helped me and comforted me.

PSALM 87

The 87th psalm is a prophecy of the holy Christian church, that it shall be a city as wide as the earth is, and in it shall be born Ethiopians, Egyptians, Babylonians, Philistines, residents of Tyre, and peoples of other lands and tongues. This shall all happen through the Gospel, which shall preach marvelous things of God, namely, the knowledge of God, how one may come to God, be freed from sin, and be saved from death, through Christ. And the worship of God in this city shall also be singing and dancing, that is, they will proclaim, praise, and thank God's grace with joy. In that city, no Moses shall plague and torment us with his law.

PSALM 87

Of the Sons of Korah. A psalm. A song.

He has set his foundation on the holy mountain; the Lord loves the gates of Zion more than all the dwellings of Jacob. Glorious things are said of you, O city of God: "I will record Rahab and Babylon among those who acknowledge me—Philistia too, and Tyre, along with Cush—and will say, 'This one was born in Zion.' "

Indeed, of Zion it will be said, "This one and that one were born in her, and the Most High himself will establish her." The Lord will write in the register of the peoples: "This one was born in Zion." As they make music they will sing, "All my fountains are in you."

PSALM 88

The 88th psalm is a psalm of prayer that prays in the person of Christ and all other great saints, lamenting the high spiritual suffering that is above all suffering, namely, the terror of God. This he calls death, the grave, and hell, as it truly is, causing miserable and pitiful conditions. St. Paul called it "the messenger of Satan" (2 Cor. 12:7) that beat on him with his fists, and "a thorn in his body" with which he was pierced (as in Greece they speared an evildoer). In like manner, the heathen slander our Lord and call him the "pierced one," while the Jews call him "the one who was hung." It is the inheritance of Christ and his people to receive this ridicule and to suffer in the world. This psalm also says that their friends and relatives, who should cry for them and suffer with them, are instead far from them.

PSALM 88

A song. A psalm of the Sons of Korah. For the director of music. According to mahalath leannoth. *A maskil of Heman the Ezrahite.*

O Lord, the God who saves me, day and night I cry out before you. May my prayer come before you; turn your ear to my cry.

For my soul is full of trouble and my life draws near the grave. I am counted among those who go down to the pit; I am like a man without strength. I am set apart with the dead, like the slain who lie in the grave, whom you remember no more, who are cut off from your care.

You have put me in the lowest pit, in the darkest depths. Your wrath lies heavily upon me; you have overwhelmed me with all your waves. You have taken from me my closest friends and have made me repulsive to them. I am confined and cannot escape; my eyes are dim with grief.

I call to you, O Lord, every day; I spread out my hands to you. Do you show your wonders to the dead? Do those who are dead rise up and praise you? Is your love declared in the grave, your faithfulness in Destruction? Are your wonders known in the place of darkness, or your righteous deeds in the land of oblivion? But I cry to you for help, O Lord; in the morning my prayer comes before you. Why, O Lord, do you reject me and hide your face from me?

From my youth I have been afflicted and close to death; I have suffered your terrors and am in despair. Your wrath has swept over me; your terrors have destroyed me. All day long they surround me like a flood; they have completely engulfed me. You have taken my companions and loved ones from me; the darkness is my closest friend.

PSALM 89

The 89th psalm is a prophecy of Christ and his kingdom. The psalmist calls it a heavenly kingdom (as Christ himself does in the Gospel). It takes up the prophecy given to David of Christ and emphasizes it with an abundant spirit. Particularly he emphasizes that this kingdom shall never, for the sake of any sin, come to an end or be left behind. Accordingly, our salvation shall not be based on our piety, although the promised kingdom of the Jews and all other earthly kingdoms last no longer or stretch no father than they are pious.

But later he begins to prophesy that such a precious and fruitful kingdom would be trampled, torn, and subverted by the Antichrist, so that it appears as though God has forgotten his former abundant promises and is doing the opposite of his own words. But this all is announced beforehand, to be a comfort to us in these last days. Therefore we should not despair, though it seems to us that there is no Christendom, no light of the church, any more on earth. And yet it always remains, however distressed, broken, and persecuted.

PSALM 89

A maskil *of Ethan the Ezrahite.*

I will sing of the Lord's great love forever; with my mouth I will make your faithfulness known through all generations. I will declare that your love stands firm forever, that you established your faithfulness in heaven itself.

You said, "I have made a covenant with my chosen one, I have sworn to David my servant, 'I will establish your line forever and make your throne firm through all generations.' "

The heavens praise your wonders, O Lord, your faithfulness too, in the assembly of the holy ones. For who in the skies above can compare with the Lord? Who is like the Lord among the heavenly beings? In the council of the holy ones God is greatly feared; he is more awesome than all who surround him. O Lord God Almighty, who is like you? You are mighty, O Lord, and your faithfulness surrounds you.

You rule over the surging sea; when its waves mount up, you still them. You crushed Rahab like one of the slain; with your strong arm you scattered your enemies. The heavens are yours, and yours also the earth; you founded the world and all that is in it. You created the north and the south; Tabor and Hermon sing for joy at your name. Your arm is endued with power; your hand is strong, your right hand exalted.

Righteousness and justice are the foundation of your throne; love and faithfulness go before you. Blessed are those who have learned to acclaim you, who walk in the light of your presence, O Lord. They rejoice in your name all day long; they exult in your righteousness. For you are their glory and strength, and by your favor you exalt our horn. Indeed, our shield belongs to the Lord, our king to the Holy One of Israel.

Once you spoke in a vision, to your faithful people you said: "I have bestowed strength on a warrior; I have exalted a young man from among the people. I have found David my servant; with my sacred oil I have anointed him. My hand will sustain him; surely my arm will strengthen him. No enemy will subject him to tribute; no wicked man will oppress him. I will crush his foes before him and strike down his adversaries. My faithful love will be with him, and through my name his horn will be exalted. I will set his hand over the sea, his right hand over the rivers. He will call out to me, 'You are my Father, my God, the Rock my Savior.' I will also appoint him my firstborn, the most exalted of the kings of the earth. I will maintain my love to him forever, and my covenant with him will never fail. I will establish his line forever, his throne as long as the heavens endure.

"If his sons forsake my law and do not follow my statutes, if they violate my decrees and fail to keep my commands, I will punish their sin with the rod, their iniquity with flogging; but I will not take my love from him, nor will I ever betray my faithfulness. I will not violate my covenant or alter what my lips have uttered. Once for all, I have sworn by my holiness—and I will not lie to David—that his line will continue forever and his throne endure before me like the sun; it will be established forever like the moon, the faithful witness in the sky.''

But you have rejected, you have spurned, you have been very angry with your anointed one. You have renounced the covenant with your servant and have defiled his crown in the dust. You have broken through all his walls and reduced his strongholds to ruins. All who pass by have plundered him; he has become the scorn of his neighbors. You have exalted the right hand of his foes; you have made all his enemies rejoice. You have turned back the edge of his sword and have not supported him in battle. You have put an end to his splendor and cast his throne to the ground. You have cut short the days of his youth; you have covered him with a mantle of shame.

How long, O Lord? Will you hide yourself forever? How long will your wrath burn like fire? Remember how fleeting is my life. For what futility you have created all men! What man can live and not see death, or save himself from the power of the grave? O Lord, where is your former great love, which in your faithfulness you swore to David? Remember, Lord, how your servant has been mocked, how I bear in my heart the taunts of all the nations, the taunts with which your enemies have mocked, O Lord, with which they have mocked every step of your anointed one.

Praise be to the Lord forever! Amen and Amen.

PSALM 90

The 90th psalm is a psalm of instruction in which Moses teaches the origin of death, namely sin, which, though known only by God and hidden from the world, is yet inborn in all from Adam to us. It shows that life here is not only short but also miserable, so that it may well be called a daily death. Nevertheless, he says that such a life is good, so that through it we would be driven to see God's grace and help to deliver us from it all. For those who never think of death and feel no misery remain senseless fools, caring nothing for God's grace or help. The psalm ends with the prayer that God would show us his work, namely his deliverance from sin and death, that is, that he would send Christ. And he asks that, while we live here, God would establish our work, that is, that both spiritual and worldly authority may be and remain favorable. A short, fine, rich, and full little prayer.

PSALM 90

A prayer of Moses the man of God.

Lord, you have been our dwelling place throughout all generations. Before the mountains were born or you brought forth the earth and the world, from everlasting to everlasting you are God.

You turn men back to dust, saying, "Return to dust, O sons of men." For a thousand years in your sight are like a day that has just gone by, or like a watch in the night. You sweep men away in the sleep of death; they are like the new grass of the morning—though in the morning it springs up new, by evening it is dry and withered.

We are consumed by your anger and terrified by your indignation. You have set our iniquities before you, our secret sins in the light of your presence. All our days pass away under your wrath; we finish our years with a moan. The length of our days is seventy years—or eighty, if we have the strength; yet their span is but trouble and sorrow, for they quickly pass, and we fly away.

Who knows the power of your anger? For your wrath is as great as the fear that is due you. Teach us to number our days aright, that we may gain a heart of wisdom.

Relent, O Lord! How long will it be? Have compassion on your servants. Satisfy us in the morning with your unfailing love, that we may sing for joy and be glad all our days. Make us glad for as many days as you have afflicted us, for as many years as we have seen trouble. May your deeds be shown to your servants, your splendor to their children.

May the favor of the Lord our God rest upon us; establish the work of our hands for us—yes, establish the work of our hands.

PSALM 91

The 91st psalm is a psalm of comfort which exhorts us to trust in God in all distress and affliction. It is full of abundant promises flowing from and spun from the first commandment. It is the second psalm in which the dear angels are proclaimed to be our guards and protectors (cf. Psalm 34), which is comforting and good to remember.

PSALM 91

He who dwells in the shelter of the Most High will rest in the shadow of the Almighty. I will say of the Lord, "He is my refuge and my fortress, my God, in whom I trust."

Surely he will save you from the fowler's snare and from the deadly pestilence. He will cover you with his feathers, and under his wings you will find refuge; his faithfulness will be your shield and rampart. You will not fear the terror of night, nor the arrow that flies by day, nor the pestilence that stalks in the darkness, nor the plague that destroys at midday. A thousand may fall at your side, ten thousand at your right hand, but it will not come near you. You will only observe with your eyes and see the punishment of the wicked.

If you make the Most High your dwelling—even the Lord, who is my refuge—then no harm will befall you, no disaster will come near your tent. For he will command his angels concerning you to guard you in all your ways; they will lift you up in their hands, so that you will not strike your foot against a stone. You will tread upon the lion and the cobra; you will trample the great lion and the serpent.

"Because he loves me," says the Lord, "I will rescue him; I will protect him, for he acknowledges my name. He will call upon me, and I will answer him; I will be with him in trouble, I will deliver him and honor him. With long life will I satisfy him and show him my salvation.''

PSALM 92

The 92nd psalm is a psalm of comfort which extols God's Word as the most highly exalted and precious gift, against the false saints, whom it attacks. They certainly flower for a time, glorious and powerful, but finally they perish. The righteous however will remain forever. Although they come to an old age, they shall yet never be old, but they become young daily through God's Word, which always conveys fruit and new growth. But fools neither consider nor understand these things, as we also see today in our own time.

PSALM 92

A psalm. A song. For the Sabbath day.

It is good to praise the Lord and make music to your name, O Most High, to proclaim your love in the morning and your faithfulness at night, to the music of the ten-stringed lyre and the melody of the harp.

For you make me glad by your deeds, O Lord; I sing for joy at the works of your hands. How great are your works, O Lord, how profound your thoughts! The senseless man does not know, fools do not understand, that though the wicked spring up like grass and all evildoers flourish, they will be forever destroyed.

But you, O Lord, are exalted forever.

For surely your enemies, O Lord, surely your enemies will perish; all evildoers will be scattered. You have exalted my horn like that of a wild ox; fine oils have been poured upon me. My eyes have seen the defeat of my adversaries; my ears have heard the rout of my wicked foes.

The righteous will flourish like a palm tree, they will grow like a cedar of Lebanon; planted in the house of the Lord, they will flourish

122

in the courts of our God. They will still bear fruit in old age, they will stay fresh and green, proclaiming, ''The Lord is upright; he is my Rock, and there is no wickedness in him.''

PSALM 93

The 93rd psalm is a prophecy of the kingdom of Christ, that it is as wide as the world and remains forever. Although floods and waters storm against it, that is, the world's death and rage oppose and struggle against it, they accomplish nothing at all. For he is greater than the world and its prince. This kingdom and all things will be ordered through his Word, without sword or armor. He will adorn his house and make it holy. For the true worship that adorns and illuminates this house is preaching, praise, and thanksgiving, which belong neither to Moses nor the Old Testament.

PSALM 93

The Lord reigns, he is robed in majesty; the Lord is robed in majesty and is armed with strength. The world is firmly established; it cannot be moved. Your throne was established long ago; you are from all eternity.

The seas have lifted up, O Lord, the seas have lifted up their voice; the seas have lifted up their pounding waves. Mightier than the thunder of the great waters, mightier than the breakers of the sea—the Lord on high is mighty.

Your statutes stand firm; holiness adorns your house for endless days, O Lord.

PSALM 94

The 94th psalm is a psalm of prayer which, by my understanding, cries out not against the heathen but against the kings and princes, priests, and prophets. He calls them fools among the people, senseless ones who teach and rule the people foolishly and badly. These are the ones who kill and persecute all the godly prophets and their disciples. As the psalmist says, they presume upon God. He has given them the power and has stood by and watched, not paying attention to those whom they slaughtered as condemned heretics and rebels. Against these authorities the psalmist prays, desiring help and support. Although he finds no help, he takes comfort in his confidence that God's Word and actions are reliable and God will not allow the corrupt throne to come upon them but will repay them for their lies and murders. Amen.

Psalm 94

O Lord, the God who avenges, O God who avenges, shine forth. Rise up, O Judge of the earth; pay back to the proud what they deserve. How long will the wicked, O Lord, how long will the wicked be jubilant?

They pour out arrogant words; all the evildoers are full of boasting. They crush your people, O Lord; they oppress your inheritance. They slay the widow and the alien; they murder the fatherless. They say, "The Lord does not see; the God of Jacob pays no heed."

Take heed, you senseless ones among the people; you fools, when will you become wise? Does he who implanted the ear not hear? Does he who formed the eye not see? Does he who disciplines nations not punish? Does he who teaches man lack knowledge? The Lord knows the thoughts of man; he knows that they are futile.

Blessed is the man you discipline, O Lord, the man you teach from your law; you grant him relief from days of trouble, till a pit is dug for the wicked. For the Lord will not reject his people; he will never forsake his inheritance. Judgment will again be founded on righteousness, and all the upright in heart will follow it.

Who will rise up for me against the wicked? Who will take a stand for me against evildoers? Unless the Lord had given me help, I would soon have dwelt in the silence of death. When I said, "My foot is slipping," your love, O Lord, supported me. When anxiety was great within me, your consolation brought joy to my soul.

Can a corrupt throne be allied with you—one that brings on misery by its decrees? They band together against the righteous and condemn the innocent to death. But the Lord has become my fortress, and my God the rock in whom I take refuge. He will repay them for their sins and destroy them for their wickedness; the Lord our God will destroy them.

PSALM 95

The 95th psalm is a prophecy of Christ; the letter to the Hebrews extensively treats it as a prophecy of the time of the New Testament and of the voice of the Gospel. In short, it teaches and calls us to Christ and to the Word of God, to true worship. He warns us by the example of the faithless fathers in the wilderness, who also did not come into the promised land on account of their unbelief and contempt for God.

You must however apply the entire psalm to Christ: He is himself the God whom we are exhorted to worship. He has made us and is our shepherd, and we are his sheep. He is the one who tested the unbelieving fathers, as Paul in 1 Cor. 10:9 also states. From henceforth he will receive no mosaic worship, but instead faith, joyful preaching, praise, and thanksgiving.

PSALM 95

Come, let us sing for joy to the Lord; let us shout aloud to the Rock of our salvation. Let us come before him with thanksgiving and extol him with music and song.

For the Lord is the great God, the great King above all gods. In his hand are the depths of the earth, and the mountain peaks belong to him. The sea is his, for he made it, and his hands formed the dry land.

Come, let us bow down in worship, let us kneel before the Lord our Maker; for he is our God and we are the people of his pasture, the flock under his care.

Today, if you hear his voice, do not harden your hearts as you did at Meribah, as you did that day at Massah in the desert, where your fathers tested and tried me, though they had seen what I did. For forty years I was angry with that generation; I said, "They are a people whose hearts go astray, and they have not known my ways." So I declared on oath in my anger, "They shall never enter my rest."

PSALM 96

The 96th psalm is a prophecy of the kingdom of Christ in all the world, in which should be nothing but joy and praise. The text is, truly, itself clear enough. In it, all the nations, lands, people, forests, seas, trees are called to worship. They should praise and thank the Lord because he judges and rules with righteousness and truth. That is, he delivers us from sin and all that sin brings with it, such as death, hell, the power of the devil, and all that is evil. This is the new song of the new kingdom from new creatures, from a new people, not born of the law nor works but born of God and Spirit. These are nothing less than miracles, done in Christ Jesus, our Lord.

PSALM 96

Sing to the Lord a new song; sing to the Lord, all the earth. Sing to the Lord, praise his name; proclaim his salvation day after day. Declare his glory among the nations, his marvelous deeds among all peoples.

For great is the Lord and most worthy of praise; he is to be feared above all gods. For all the gods of the nations are idols, but the Lord made the heavens. Splendor and majesty are before him; strength and glory are in his sanctuary.

Ascribe to the Lord, O families of nations, ascribe to the Lord glory and strength. Ascribe to the Lord the glory due his name; bring an offering and come into his courts. Worship the Lord in the splendor of his holiness; tremble before him, all the earth.

Say among the nations, "The Lord reigns." The world is firmly established, it cannot be moved; he will judge the peoples with equity. Let the heavens rejoice, let the earth be glad; let the sea resound, and all that is in it; let the fields be jubilant, and everything in them. Then all the trees of the forest will sing for joy; they will sing before the Lord, for he comes, he comes to judge the earth. He will judge the world in righteousness and the peoples in his truth.

PSALM 97

The 97th psalm is a prophecy of the kingdom of Christ, just as the preceding psalm was. And the significance is always this, that Christ rules and maintains this kingdom through the Gospel, through which he sends out thunder and lightnings and burns his enemies and melts the mountains. That is, he brings low all holiness, all wisdom, power, and whatever is great so that they might be holy, wise, great, and powerful through him alone, and not otherwise. Along with these enemies and mountains, the Jewish kingdom and worship perish also, as well as all which is not Christ. For he alone shall endure, and all others pass away, as the stone in Daniel, cut from the mountain, fills the whole world and scatters everything else and makes them to nothing (Dan. 2:34). He will be the mountain filling the whole world.

PSALM 97

The Lord reigns, let the earth be glad; let the distant shores rejoice.

Clouds and thick darkness surround him; righteousness and justice are the foundation of his throne. Fire goes before him and consumes his foes on every side. His lightning lights up the world; the earth sees and trembles. The mountains melt like wax before the Lord, before the Lord of all the earth. The heavens proclaim his righteousness, and all the peoples see his glory.

All who worship images are put to shame, those who boast in idols— worship him, all you gods!

Zion hears and rejoices and the villages of Judah are glad because of your judgments, O Lord. For you, O Lord, are the Most High over all the earth; you are exalted far above all gods.

Let those who love the Lord hate evil, for he guards the lives of his faithful ones and delivers them from the hand of the wicked. Light is shed upon the righteous and joy on the upright in heart. Rejoice in the Lord, you who are righteous, and praise his holy name.

PSALM 98

The 98th psalm, like the preceding psalm, is a prophecy of the kingdom of Christ, which extends into all the world. It also calls us to be joyful and to praise God for his salvation, that is, preach and give thanks for the redemption given us through Christ. Here then is worship—not offerings given in Jerusalem, but preaching and thanksgiving that he is king in righteousness over all the world, that is, that he has redeemed us from sin and death by himself alone, without our merits.

PSALM 98

A psalm.

Sing to the Lord a new song, for he has done marvelous things; his right hand and his holy arm have worked salvation for him. The Lord has made his salvation known and revealed his righteousness to the nations. He has remembered his love and his faithfulness to the house of Israel; all the ends of the earth have seen the salvation of our God.

Shout for joy to the Lord, all the earth, burst into jubilant song with music; make music to the Lord with the harp, with the harp and the sound of singing, with trumpets and the blast of the ram's horn— shout for joy before the Lord, the King.

Let the sea resound, and everything in it, the world, and all who live in it. Let the rivers clap their hands, let the mountains sing together for joy; let them sing before the Lord, for he comes to judge the earth. He will judge the world in righteousness and the peoples with equity.

PSALM 99

The 99th psalm is a psalm of instruction which exhorts the people of Israel to praise their God in Zion—in spite of the fact that the nations rage against them because they are a special people of God before all others. They suffer much on that account. The psalmist praises Moses, Aaron, and Samuel, who were the chief among the people of Israel. However (as the words declare) he also teaches the people of Israel themselves that they should know that true worship consists not in the sacrifice of many cattle, but rather in knowing God's wonders and giving him thanks for making them godly and redeeming them from sin. This psalm is also a prophecy of Christ, who rules the true Zion in all the world and has established his throne of grace and his footstool in heaven, on account of which all the world is now angry, raving, and foolish and persecutes and kills the Christians.

PSALM 99

The Lord reigns, let the nations tremble; he sits enthroned between the cherubim, let the earth shake. Great is the Lord in Zion; he is exalted over all the nations. Let them praise your great and awesome name—he is holy.

The King is mighty, he loves justice—you have established equity; in Jacob you have done what is just and right. Exalt the Lord our God and worship at his footstool; he is holy.

Moses and Aaron were among his priests, Samuel was among those who called on his name; they called on the Lord and he answered them. He spoke to them from the pillar of cloud; they kept his statutes and the decrees he gave them.

O Lord our God, you answered them; you were to Israel a forgiving God, though you punished their misdeeds. Exalt the Lord our God and worship at his holy mountain, for the Lord our God is holy.

PSALM 100

The 100th psalm is a prophecy of Christ. It calls on all the world to be joyful, praise, and give thanks, that is, to worship God and come to his throne and his courts, and to call on him with all confidence. For his grace is an eternal kingdom, which truly remains forever and ever.

PSALM 100

A psalm. For giving thanks.

Shout for joy to the Lord, all the earth. Worship the Lord with gladness; come before him with joyful songs. Know that the Lord is God. It is he who made us, and we are his; we are his people, the sheep of his pasture.

Enter his gates with thanksgiving and his courts with praise; give thanks to him and praise his name. For the Lord is good and his love endures forever; his faithfulness continues through all generations.

PSALM 101

The 101st psalm is a psalm of instruction in which David uses himself as an example of how to have godly helpers and not tolerate evil servants. He accordingly lists the various lusts and vices of an evil worker, which belongs in a longer commentary to explain. This he calls "singing of love and justice," that is, singing of how God is gracious to the godly and punishes the wicked and how every worker should be doing good and shunning evil. How it shall go with them on these accounts is well depicted in Absalom, Ahithophel, Joab, and others. For whoever wants to make and keep the people godly shall be burdened with all hatred and envy. Therefore he may well sing to God and give him thanks who has given grace and justice to him. For where God does not give this, such a song would remain unsung. In its place only cursing and scolding would remain in the house and the only hope be hanging and beheadings and the like.

PSALM 101

Of David. A psalm.

I will sing of your love and justice; to you, O Lord, I will sing praise. I will be careful to lead a blameless life—when will you come to me?

I will walk in my house with blameless heart. I will set before my eyes no vile thing.

The deeds of faithless men I hate; they will not cling to me. Men of perverse heart shall be far from me; I will have nothing to do with evil.

Whoever slanders his neighbor in secret, him will I put to silence; whoever has haughty eyes and a proud heart, him will I not endure.

My eyes will be on the faithful in the land, that they may dwell with me; he whose walk is blameless will minister to me.

No one who practices deceit will dwell in my house; no one who speaks falsely will stand in my presence.

Every morning I will put to silence all the wicked in the land; I will cut off every evildoer from the city of the Lord.

PSALM 102

The 102nd psalm is a psalm of prayer. In it the fathers of old—weary of laws, of sins, and of death—wholeheartedly yearn and call for the kingdom of grace, promised in Christ. They ask that God yet again build up Zion and set in place her stones and dust, that he would yet again enter in and let his glory be seen in all kingdoms, that he would rescue his captives from sin and death so that they may come together and thank him—that is, that they may worship him in the true Zion—and the Old Testament come to an end.

For without Christ there is indeed nothing but strength broken in the middle of life and days cut short, that is, a miserable, short, wretched life from which the psalmist is reluctantly removed. But in his kingdom is eternal life, and his time has no end. He is the one who was before heaven and earth and made them and will again change and renew them. Therefore he is outside of and over all time. His year has no end and there is no dying there. This kingdom (he says) we will gladly receive. May such a kingdom, your kingdom, come! Amen.

PSALM 102

A prayer of an afflicted man. When he is faint and pours out his lament before the Lord.

Hear my prayer, O Lord; let my cry for help come to you. Do not hide your face from me when I am in distress. Turn your ear to me; when I call, answer me quickly.

For my days vanish like smoke; my bones burn like glowing embers. My heart is blighted and withered like grass; I forget to eat my food. Because of my loud groaning I am reduced to skin and bones. I am like a desert owl, like an owl among the ruins. I lie awake; I have become like a bird alone on a roof. All day long my enemies taunt me; those who rail against me use my name as a curse. For I eat ashes as my food and mingle my drink with tears because of your great wrath, for you have taken me up and thrown me aside. My days are like the evening shadow; I wither away like grass.

But you, O Lord, sit enthroned forever; your renown endures through all generations. You will arise and have compassion on Zion, for it is time to show favor to her; the appointed time has come. For her stones are dear to your servants; her very dust moves them to pity. The nations will fear the name of the Lord, all the kings of the earth will revere your glory. For the Lord will rebuild Zion and appear in his glory. He will respond to the prayer of the destitute; he will not despise their plea.

Let this be written for a future generation, that a people not yet created may praise the Lord: "The Lord looked down from his sanctuary on high, from heaven he viewed the earth, to hear the groans of the prisoners and release those condemned to death." So the name of the Lord will be declared in Zion and his praise in Jerusalem when the peoples and the kingdoms assemble to worship the Lord.

In the course of my life he broke my strength; he cut short my days. So I said: "Do not take me away, O my God, in the midst of my days; your years go on through all generations. In the beginning you laid the foundations of the earth, and the heavens are the work of your hands. They will perish, but you remain; they will all wear out like a garment. Like clothing you will change them and they will be discarded. But you remain the same, and your years will never end. The children of your servants will live in your presence; their descendants will be established before you.''

PSALM 103

Psalm 103 is a psalm of thanks, beautifully and lovingly made, in which the psalmist thanks God for all his goodness, namely, forgiveness of sins, making a sound body and soul, giving us enough of all sorts of goods, making us joyful and confident, delivering us from enemies and distress. In short, he thanks God that he is a gracious, compassionate, and loving Father toward us, though we are frail and unsteady creatures. God does not deal with us according to our sins, but according to his gracious goodness to us, who acknowledge him and keep his covenant. That is, we believe in him and gladly will be godly and neither arrogant nor stiff necked in our holiness and righteousness (which would indeed be a striving directly contrary to the covenant, especially the first commandment).

This all comes to pass in Christ, who for this reason was promised and now is come, whose kingdom reigns over all. For at the end, where he calls on the angels, mighty ones, servants hosts, to give him praise and let his Word be heard, I am of the opinion that the psalm is speaking of Christ and his apostles, Gospel, and church—where such grace rules; for what we need and what saves us all comes to pass in Christ and not outside of him.

PSALM 103

Of David.

Praise the Lord, O my soul; all my inmost being, praise his holy name. Praise the Lord, O my soul, and forget not all his benefits—who forgives all your sins and heals all your diseases, who redeems your life from the pit and crowns you with love and compassion, who satisfies your desires with good things so that your youth is renewed like the eagle's.

The Lord works righteousness and justice for all the oppressed.

He made known his ways to Moses, his deeds to the people of Israel: The Lord is compassionate and gracious, slow to anger, abounding in love. He will not always accuse, nor will he harbor his anger forever; he does not treat us as our sins deserve or repay us according to our iniquities. For as high as the heavens are above the earth, so great is his love for those who fear him; as far as the east is from the west, so far has he removed our transgressions from us. As a father has compassion on his children, so the Lord has compassion on those who fear him; for he knows how we are formed, he remembers that we are dust. As for man, his days are like grass, he flourishes like a flower of the field; the wind blows over it and it is gone, and its place remembers it no more. But from everlasting to everlasting the Lord's love is with those who fear him, and his righteousness with their children's children—with those who keep his covenant and remember to obey his precepts.

The Lord has established his throne in heaven, and his kingdom rules over all.

Praise the Lord, you his angels, you mighty ones who do his bidding, who obey his word. Praise the Lord, all his heavenly hosts, you his servants who do his will. Praise the Lord, all his works everywhere in his dominion.

Praise the Lord, O my soul.

PSALM 104

The 104th psalm is a psalm of thanks for all the works that God had accomplished in heaven and on earth, beyond those done for us here on earth. He has surely ordered all things according to a wise plan to produce works, fruits, and crops. The psalmist recounts these one after the other: the heavens—full of light and outstretched as a tapestry without posts or rafters; the clouds—an arch without foundation or pillar; the wind flying without wings; the angels going and coming, appearing like a wind or a flame.

Thus sings the palmist. He finds his desires and joy in the creations of God, which are so wonderfully made and so beautifully ordered together. But who pays attention to this or sees that this is so? Only faith and the Spirit.

PSALM 104

Praise the Lord, O my soul.

O Lord my God, you are very great; you are clothed with splendor and majesty. He wraps himself in light as with a garment; he stretches out the heavens like a tent and lays the beams of his upper chambers on their waters. He makes the clouds his chariot and rides on the wings of the wind. He makes winds his messengers, flames of fire his servants.

He set the earth on its foundations; it can never be moved. You covered it with the deep as with a garment; the waters stood above the mountains. But at your rebuke the waters fled, at the sound of your thunder they took to flight; they flowed over the mountains, they went down into the valleys, to the place you assigned for them. You set a boundary they cannot cross; never again will they cover the earth.

He makes springs pour water into the ravines; it flows between the mountains. They give water to all the beasts of the field; the wild donkeys quench their thirst. The birds of the air nest by the waters; they sing among the branches. He waters the mountains from his upper chambers; the earth is satisfied by the fruit of his work. He makes grass grow for the cattle, and plants for man to cultivate— bringing forth food from the earth: wine that gladdens the heart of man, oil to make his face shine, and bread that sustains his heart. The trees of the Lord are well watered, the cedars of Lebanon that he planted. There the birds make their nests; the stork has its home in the pine trees. The high mountains belong to the wild goats; the crags are a refuge for the coneys.

The moon marks off the seasons, and the sun knows when to go down. You bring darkness, it becomes night, and all the beasts of the forest prowl. The lions roar for their prey and seek their food from God. The sun rises, and they steal away; they return and lie down in their dens. Then man goes out to his work, to his labor until evening.

How many are your works, O Lord! In wisdom you made them all; the earth is full of your creatures. There is the sea, vast and spacious, teeming with creatures beyond number—living things both large and small. There the ships go to and fro, and the leviathan, which you formed to frolic there.

These all look to you to give them their food at the proper time. When you give it to them, they gather it up; when you open your hand, they are satisfied with good things. When you hide your face, they are terrified; when you take away their breath, they die and return to the dust. When you send your Spirit, they are created, and you renew the face of the earth.

May the glory of the Lord endure forever; may the Lord rejoice in his works—he who looks at the earth, and it trembles, who touches the mountains, and they smoke.

I will sing to the Lord all my life; I will sing praise to my God as long as I live. May my meditation be pleasing to him, as I rejoice in the Lord. But may sinners vanish from the earth and the wicked be no more.

Praise the Lord, O my soul.

Praise the Lord.

PSALM 105

The 105th psalm is a psalm of thanks in which the people of Israel give thanks for all the miracles of old that God had done from Abraham on, until they were brought into the land of Canaan. He then recounts them all one after another. He concludes as Moses did (Deut. 9:4–6), noting that God had not done such wonders on account of their goodness or merit, but for the sake of his covenant and promises that he had spoken to Abraham. How pious they really were and what they truly deserved is shown in the following psalm.

PSALM 105

Give thanks to the Lord, call on his name; make known among the nations what he has done. Sing to him, sing praise to him; tell of all his wonderful acts. Glory in his holy name; let the hearts of those who seek the Lord rejoice. Look to the Lord and his strength; seek his face always.

Remember the wonders he has done, his miracles, and the judgments he pronounced, O descendants of Abraham his servant, O sons of Jacob, his chosen ones. He is the Lord our God; his judgments are in all the earth.

He remembers his covenant forever, the word he commanded, for a thousand generations, the covenant he made with Abraham, the oath he swore to Isaac. He confirmed it to Jacob as a decree, to Israel as an everlasting covenant: "To you I will give the land of Canaan as the portion you will inherit."

When they were but few in number, few indeed, and strangers in it, they wandered from nation to nation, from one kingdom to another. He allowed no one to oppress them; for their sake he rebuked kings: "Do not touch my anointed ones; do my prophets no harm."

He called down famine on the land and destroyed all their supplies of food; and he sent a man before them—Joseph, sold as a slave. They bruised his feet with shackles, his neck was put in irons, till what he foretold came to pass, till the word of the Lord proved him true. The king sent and released him, the ruler of peoples set him free. He made him master of his household, ruler over all he possessed, to instruct his princes as he pleased and teach his elders wisdom.

Then Israel entered Egypt; Jacob lived as an alien in the land of Ham. The Lord made his people very fruitful; he made them too numerous for their foes, whose hearts he turned to hate his people, to conspire against his servants. He sent Moses his servant, and Aaron, whom he had chosen. They performed his miraculous signs among them, his wonders in the land of Ham. He sent darkness and made the land dark—for had they not rebelled against his words? He turned their waters into blood, causing their fish to die. Their land teemed with frogs, which went up into the bedrooms of their rulers. He spoke, and there came swarms of flies, and gnats throughout their country. He turned their rain into hail, with lightning throughout their land; he struck down their vines and fig trees and shattered the trees of their country. He spoke, and the locusts came, grasshoppers without number; they ate up every green thing in their land, ate up the produce of their soil. Then he struck down all the firstborn in their land, the firstfruits of all their manhood.

He brought out Israel, laden with silver and gold, and from among their tribes no one faltered. Egypt was glad when they left, because dread of Israel had fallen on them. He spread out a cloud as a covering, and a fire to give light at night. They asked, and he brought them quail and satisfied them with the bread of heaven. He opened the rock, and water gushed out; like a river it flowed in the desert.

For he remembered his holy promise given to his servant Abraham. He brought out his people with rejoicing, his chosen ones with shouts of joy; he gave them the lands of the nations, and they fell heir to what others had toiled for—that they might keep his precepts and observe his laws.

Praise the Lord.

PSALM 106

The 106th psalm is a psalm of thanks in which the psalmist acknowledges all the sins that the people of Israel had committed against God, by which they had made themselves unworthy for all his grace and blessings. Therefore it says constantly that God has done all these things for his name's sake and for the remembrance of his covenant. Moses also says this (Deut. 9:6), therefore they cannot glory in themselves except in His grace alone—as we also can have no other glory.

PSALM 106

Praise the Lord.

Give thanks to the Lord, for he is good; his love endures forever. Who can proclaim the mighty acts of the Lord or fully declare his praise? Blessed are they who maintain justice, who constantly do what is right. Remember me, O Lord, when you show favor to your people, come to my aid when you save them, that I may enjoy the prosperity of your chosen ones, that I may share in the joy of your nation and join your inheritance in giving praise.

We have sinned, even as our fathers did; we have done wrong and acted wickedly. When our fathers were in Egypt, they gave no thought to your miracles; they did not remember your many kindnesses, and they rebelled by the sea, the Red Sea. Yet he saved them for his name's sake, to make his mighty power known. He rebuked the Red Sea, and it dried up; he led them through the depths as through a desert. He saved them from the hand of the foe; from the hand of the enemy he redeemed them. The waters covered their adversaries; not one of them survived. Then they believed his promises and sang his praise.

But they soon forgot what he had done and did not wait for his counsel. In the desert they gave in to their craving; in the wasteland they put God to the test. So he gave them what they asked for, but sent a wasting disease upon them.

In the camp they grew envious of Moses and of Aaron, who was consecrated to the Lord. The earth opened up and swallowed Dathan; it buried the company of Abiram. Fire blazed among their followers; a flame consumed the wicked.

At Horeb they made a calf and worshiped an idol cast from metal. They exchanged their Glory for an image of a bull, which eats grass. They forgot the God who saved them, who had done great things in Egypt, miracles in the land of Ham and awesome deeds by the Red Sea. So he said he would destroy them—had not Moses, his chosen one, stood in the breach before him to keep his wrath from destroying them.

Then they despised the pleasant land; they did not believe his promise. They grumbled in their tents and did not obey the Lord. So he swore to them with uplifted hand that he would make them fall in the desert, make their descendants fall among the nations and scatter them throughout the lands.

They yoked themselves to the Baal of Peor and ate sacrifices offered to lifeless gods; they provoked the Lord to anger by their wicked deeds, and a plague broke out among them. But Phinehas stood up and intervened, and the plague was checked. This was credited to him as righteousness for endless generations to come. By the waters of Meribah they angered the Lord, and trouble came to Moses because of them; for they rebelled against the Spirit of God, and rash words came from Moses' lips.

They did not destroy the peoples as the Lord had commanded them, but they mingled with the nations and adopted their customs. They worshiped their idols, which became a snare to them. They sacrificed their sons and their daughters to demons. They shed innocent blood, the blood of their sons and daughters, whom they sacrificed to the idols of Canaan, and the land was desecrated by their blood. They defiled themselves by what they did; by their deeds they prostituted themselves.

Therefore the Lord was angry with his people and abhorred his inheritance. He handed them over to the nations, and their foes ruled over them. Their enemies oppressed them and subjected them to their power. Many times he delivered them, but they were bent on rebellion and they wasted away in their sin.

But he took note of their distress when he heard their cry; for their sake he remembered his covenant and out of his great love he relented. He caused them to be pitied by all who held them captive.

Save us, O Lord our God, and gather us from the nations, that we may give thanks to your holy name and glory in your praise.

Praise be to the Lord, the God of Israel, from everlasting to everlasting. Let all the people say, ''Amen!''

Praise the Lord.

PSALM 107

The 107th psalm is a psalm of thanks for the help that God shows to all people in their distress, whether they are Gentile or Jew. This help the heathen have sought by various idols and we Christians and Turks have sought by various saints up until now (and to a great extent still do): "St. Leonard has released the prisoners, St. Bastian delivers from pestilence, St. George protects in battle, St. Erasmus makes one rich, and St. Christopher has become the god of sea and water." We have thus divided all of God's help among the saints, as the heathen among their idols, and have stolen and robbed from God—to whom alone this psalm is dedicated and whom alone the psalm calls on us to thank.

PSALM 107

Give thanks to the Lord, for he is good; his love endures forever. Let the redeemed of the Lord say this—those he redeemed from the hand of the foe, those he gathered from the lands, from east and west, from north and south.

Some wandered in desert wastelands, finding no way to a city where they could settle. They were hungry and thirsty, and their lives ebbed away. Then they cried out to the Lord in their trouble, and he delivered them from their distress. He led them by a straight way to a city where they could settle. Let them give thanks to the Lord for his unfailing love and his wonderful deeds for men, for he satisfies the thirsty and fills the hungry with good things.

Some sat in darkness and the deepest gloom, prisoners suffering in iron chains, for they had rebelled against the words of God and despised the counsel of the Most High. So he subjected them to bitter labor; they stumbled, and there was no one to help. Then they cried to the Lord in their trouble, and he saved them from their distress. He brought them out of darkness and the deepest gloom and broke away their chains. Let them give thanks to the Lord for his unfailing love and his wonderful deeds for men, for he breaks down gates of bronze and cuts through bars of iron.

Some became fools through their rebellious ways and suffered affliction because of their iniquities. They loathed all food and drew near the gates of death. Then they cried to the Lord in their trouble, and he saved them from their distress. He sent forth his word and healed them; he rescued them from the grave. Let them give thanks to the Lord for his unfailing love and his wonderful deeds for men. Let them sacrifice thank offerings and tell of his works with songs of joy.

Others went out on the sea in ships; they were merchants on the mighty waters. They saw the works of the Lord, his wonderful deeds in the deep. For he spoke and stirred up a tempest that lifted high the waves. They mounted up to the heavens and went down to the depths; in their peril their courage melted away. They reeled and staggered like drunken men; they were at their wits' end. Then they cried out to the Lord in their trouble, and he brought them out of their distress. He stilled the storm to a whisper; the waves of the sea were hushed. They were glad when it grew calm, and he guided them to their desired haven. Let them give thanks to the Lord for his unfailing love and his wonderful deeds for men. Let them exalt him in the assembly of the people and praise him in the council of the elders.

He turned rivers into a desert, flowing springs into thirsty ground, and fruitful land into a salt waste, because of the wickedness of those who lived there. He turned the desert into pools of water and the parched ground into flowing springs; there he brought the hungry to live, and they founded a city where they could settle. They sowed fields and planted vineyards that yielded a fruitful harvest; he blessed them, and their numbers greatly increased, and he did not let their herds diminish.

Then their numbers decreased, and they were humbled by oppression, calamity and sorrow; he who pours contempt on nobles made them wander in a trackless waste. But he lifted the needy out of their affliction and increased their families like flocks. The upright see and rejoice, but all the wicked shut their mouths.

Whoever is wise, let him heed these things and consider the great love of the Lord.

PSALM 108

The 108th psalm is a psalm of thanks, with words almost like Psalm 60, in which the psalmist gives thanks for God's kingdom. Already in the first verse, the psalm exalts the kingdom of Christ and prays that God will establish his kingdom in all the world and accordingly bring David's kingdom to its proper, final, full station. For David had only a slight, partial piece (compared to the whole world) of that which was promised to come to him. As Is. 9:7 also says, "He will reign on the throne of David and over his kingdom."

PSALM 108

A song. A psalm of David.

My heart is steadfast, O God; I will sing and make music with all my soul. Awake, harp and lyre! I will awaken the dawn. I will praise you, O Lord, among the nations; I will sing of you among the peoples. For great is your love, higher than the heavens; your faithfulness reaches to the skies. Be exalted, O God, above the heavens, and let your glory be over all the earth.

Save us and help us with your right hand, that those you love may be delivered. God has spoken from his sanctuary: "In triumph I will parcel out Shechem and measure off the Valley of Succoth. Gilead is mine, Manasseh is mine; Ephraim is my helmet, Judah my scepter. Moab is my washbasin, upon Edom I toss my sandal; over Philistia I shout in triumph."

Who will bring me to the fortified city? Who will lead me to Edom? Is it not you, O God, you who have rejected us and no longer go out with our armies? Give us aid against the enemy, for the help of man is worthless. With God we will gain the victory, and he will trample down our enemies.

PSALM 109

The 109th psalm is a psalm of prayer, prayed in the person of Christ against Judas, his betrayer, and against the Jews, his crucifiers.

[From Luther's commentary on four psalms of comfort:] In Acts 1:20, St. Peter applied this psalm to Judas when they were selecting Matthias to replace him. He did not mean to say that the psalm speaks only about Judas. . . .

The psalm begins with Judas and then extends to everyone of Judas' ilk, to all schismatics and persecutors of the Word of Christ; for they always slander the truth and persecute the genuine Christians. (Luther's Works, American Edition 14:257)

[From Luther's lectures on Gen. 39:13–15:] Christ himself complains of these matters in Ps. 109:2. . . . For thus the enemies of the truth are accustomed to obscure, traduce, and corrupt the fruits and gains of the Gospel and of salvation among simple and godly hearers. . . . [These enemies] adorn themselves with false and counterfeit praises; but they defame us, in order to make us more obnoxious to those who are strangers to our doctrine. (Luther's Works, American Edition 7:92)

PSALM 109

For the director of music. Of David. A psalm.

O God, whom I praise, do not remain silent, for wicked and deceitful men have opened their mouths against me; they have spoken against me with lying tongues. With words of hatred they surround me; they attack me without cause. In return for my friendship they accuse me, but I am a man of prayer. They repay me evil for good, and hatred for my friendship.

Appoint an evil man to oppose him; let an accuser stand at his right hand. When he is tried, let him be found guilty, and may his prayers condemn him. May his days be few; may another take his place of leadership. May his children be fatherless and his wife a widow. May his children be wandering beggars; may they be driven from their ruined homes. May a creditor seize all he has; may strangers plunder the fruits of his labor. May no one extend kindness to him or take pity on his fatherless children. May his descendants be cut off, their names blotted out from the next generation. May the iniquity of his fathers be remembered before the Lord; may the sin of his mother never be blotted out. May their sins always remain before the Lord, that he may cut off the memory of them from the earth.

For he never thought of doing a kindness, but hounded to death the poor and the needy and the brokenhearted. He loved to pronounce a curse—may it come on him; he found no pleasure in blessing—may it be far from him. He wore cursing as his garment; it entered into his body like water, into his bones like oil. May it be like a cloak wrapped about him, like a belt tied forever around him. May this be the Lord's payment to my accusers, to those who speak evil of me.

But you, O Sovereign Lord, deal well with me for your name's sake; out of the goodness of your love, deliver me. For I am poor and needy, and my heart is wounded within me. I fade away like an evening shadow; I am shaken off like a locust. My knees give way from fasting; my body is thin and gaunt. I am an object of scorn to my accusers; when they see me, they shake their heads.

Help me, O Lord my God; save me in accordance with your love. Let them know that it is your hand, that you, O Lord, have done it. They may curse, but you will bless; when they attack they will be put to shame, but your servant will rejoice. My accusers will be clothed with disgrace and wrapped in shame as in a cloak.

With my mouth I will greatly extol the Lord; in the great throng I will praise him. For he stands at the right hand of the needy one, to save his life from those who condemn him.

PSALM 110

The 110th psalm is a prophecy of Christ, that he shall be an eternal king and priest, indeed true God, sitting at the right hand of God, and that he would be glorified and recognized. In the entire Scripture there is nothing like this psalm. It would be right to acknowledge it as the chief confirmation of the Christian faith. For nowhere else is Christ prophesied with such clear, plain words as a priest and an eternal priest. It is prophesied as well that the priesthood of Aaron would be abolished. This psalm is yet again and more splendidly extolled in the epistle to the Hebrews. It is indeed a shame that such a psalm is not more richly extolled by Christians.

PSALM 110

Of David. A psalm.

The Lord says to my Lord: "Sit at my right hand until I make your enemies a footstool for your feet."

The Lord will extend your mighty scepter from Zion; rule in the midst of your enemies. Your troops will be willing on your day of battle. Arrayed in holy majesty, from the womb of the dawn you will receive the dew of your youth.

The Lord has sworn and will not change his mind: "You are a priest forever, in the order of Melchizedek."

The Lord is at your right hand; he will crush kings on the day of his wrath. He will judge the nations, heaping up the dead and crushing the rulers of the whole earth. He will drink from a brook beside the way; therefore he will lift up his head.

PSALM 111

The 111th psalm is a psalm of thanks for the people of Israel to sing at the Passover, concerning the Passover lamb. In this psalm they learn to praise God and give thanks in a fine, short song for all his wonderful works, especially for the spiritual authority, priesthood, Passover, law, God's Word, freedom, justice, the land, God's help, and other blessings.

PSALM 111

Praise the Lord.

I will extol the Lord with all my heart in the council of the upright and in the assembly.

Great are the works of the Lord; they are pondered by all who delight in them. Glorious and majestic are his deeds, and his righteousness endures forever. He has caused his wonders to be remembered; the Lord is gracious and compassionate. He provides food for those who fear him; he remembers his covenant forever. He has shown his people the power of his works, giving them the lands of other nations. The works of his hands are faithful and just; all his precepts are trustworthy. They are steadfast for ever and ever, done in faithfulness and uprightness. He provided redemption for his people; he ordained his covenant forever—holy and awesome is his name.

The fear of the Lord is the beginning of wisdom; all who follow his precepts have good understanding. To him belongs eternal praise.

PSALM 112

The 112th psalm is a psalm of comfort in which the pious, who fear God, are praised for their good life and are promised eternal comfort against all trouble. They are especially commended to a sincere confidence and trust in God's grace, so that they may be undismayed and undaunted (which is the real, true faith) until they see the destruction of the godless and their foes.

PSALM 112

Praise the Lord.

Blessed is the man who fears the Lord, who finds great delight in his commands.

His children will be mighty in the land; the generation of the upright will be blessed. Wealth and riches are in his house, and his righteousness endures forever. Even in darkness light dawns for the upright, for the gracious and compassionate and righteous man. Good will come to him who is generous and lends freely, who conducts his affairs with justice. Surely he will never be shaken; a righteous man will be remembered forever. He will have no fear of bad news; his heart is steadfast, trusting in the Lord. His heart is secure, he will have no fear; in the end he will look in triumph on his foes. He has scattered abroad his gifts to the poor, his righteousness endures forever; his horn will be lifted high in honor.

The wicked man will see and be vexed, he will gnash his teeth and waste away; the longings of the wicked will come to nothing.

PSALM 113

The 113th psalm is a prophecy of the kingdom of Christ, which from the rising of the sun to its setting shall extend over all the nations. It calls on all nations to praise God and proclaim his grace. For he is a God of the poor and the troubled, a delightful God and worthy of our grace, who sits on high and loves and exalts the humble. For this is Christ's office and work in his kingdom: to humble the exalted, to make foolish the wise, to damn the holy, to wither the fruitful, and on the other hand to exalt the humble, to make holy the sinner, and to make the barren into a joyful mother of children.

PSALM 113

Praise the Lord.

Praise, O servants of the Lord, praise the name of the Lord. Let the name of the Lord be praised, both now and forevermore. From the rising of the sun to the place where it sets, the name of the Lord is to be praised.

The Lord is exalted over all the nations, his glory above the heavens. Who is like the Lord our God, the One who sits enthroned on high, who stoops down to look on the heavens and the earth?

He raises the poor from the dust and lifts the needy from the ash heap; he seats them with princes, with the princes of their people. He settles the barren woman in her home as a happy mother of children.

Praise the Lord.

PSALM 114

The 114th psalm is a psalm of thanks, for the people of Israel to praise God at Passover for his wonderful works. He had led them out of Egypt, through the Red Sea, through the dry wilderness, mountains, and the Jordan, into the promised land. We sing this psalm daily to Christ to praise him who has led us out of death and sin, through the wilderness of the flesh and the devil, into an eternal life.

PSALM 114

When Israel came out of Egypt, the house of Jacob from a people of foreign tongue, Judah became God's sanctuary, Israel his dominion.

The sea looked and fled, the Jordan turned back; the mountains skipped like rams, the hills like lambs.

Why was it, O sea, that you fled, O Jordan, that you turned back, you mountains, that you skipped like rams, you hills, like lambs?

Tremble, O earth, at the presence of the Lord, at the presence of the God of Jacob, who turned the rock into a pool, the hard rock into springs of water.

PSALM 115

The 115th psalm is a psalm of thanks in which God is praised that he is the true helping God. All other gods are vain idols that cannot help us. Therefore we pray in verse 1, "Not to us, O Lord . . . ," that is, do not look at how religious and respectable we are, lest you no longer help us, and we become like the heathen, a people without God, or again, as those who have a helpless god, as they accuse us. But rather look to your glory and to your name, that you are called and reputed to be a true living God abundant in help. For your name's sake come with us, not for our name's sake—that we are called God's servants, workers, singers, fasters, and well-doers—for such names the heathen also can have and are of no help.

PSALM 115

Not to us, O Lord, not to us but to your name be the glory, because of your love and faithfulness.

Why do the nations say, "Where is their God?" Our God is in heaven; he does whatever pleases him. But their idols are silver and gold, made by the hands of men. They have mouths, but cannot speak, eyes, but they cannot see; they have ears, but cannot hear, noses, but they cannot smell; they have hands, but cannot feel, feet, but they cannot walk; nor can they utter a sound with their throats. Those who make them will be like them, and so will all who trust in them.

O house of Israel, trust in the Lord—he is their help and shield. O house of Aaron, trust in the Lord—he is their help and shield. You who fear him, trust in the Lord—he is their help and shield.

The Lord remembers us and will bless us: He will bless the house of Israel, he will bless the house of Aaron, he will bless those who fear the Lord—small and great alike.

May the Lord make you increase, both you and your children. May you be blessed by the Lord, the Maker of heaven and earth.

The highest heavens belong to the Lord, but the earth he has given to man. It is not the dead who praise the Lord, those who go down to silence; it is we who extol the Lord, both now and forevermore.

Praise the Lord.

PSALM 116

The 116th psalm is a psalm of thanks in which the psalmist is joyful and gives thanks that God has heard his prayer and has rescued him from the distress of death and the anguish of hell. Like several other psalms above, it speaks of the deep spiritual affliction, of which few people know.

He also laments in this psalm that things are so bad, yet he confesses his faith and the truth of God. He calls all human holiness, virtue, and confidence only falsehood and emptiness. This the world will not and cannot hear nor tolerate. Thus it comes that the godly suffer, tremble, and fear all kinds of misfortune.

But despite all, he is comforted by this, that God's Word is true and will only motivate us the more: "They give me to drink from the cup of their wrath. All right, then I will take the cup of grace and salvation and drink myself spiritually drunk and (through preaching) pour out from this cup on those who will drink with me and who draw their grace from the Word." This is our cup, and with this cup we will worship God and praise his name. We will fulfill our vows, namely the first commandment, that we receive him as the one God and praise him as the only God worthy to preach and to be called upon. You find here also that giving thanks, preaching, and confessing God's name before all people is the true worship of God.

PSALM 116

I love the Lord, for he heard my voice; he heard my cry for mercy. Because he turned his ear to me, I will call on him as long as I live.

The cords of death entangled me, the anguish of the grave came upon me; I was overcome by trouble and sorrow. Then I called on the name of the Lord: "O Lord, save me!"

The Lord is gracious and righteous; our God is full of compassion. The Lord protects the simplehearted; when I was in great need, he saved me.

Be at rest once more, O my soul, for the Lord has been good to you.

For you, O Lord, have delivered my soul from death, my eyes from tears, my feet from stumbling, that I may walk before the Lord in the land of the living. I believed; therefore I said, "I am greatly afflicted." And in my dismay I said, "All men are liars."

How can I repay the Lord for all his goodness to me? I will lift up the cup of salvation and call on the name of the Lord. I will fulfill my vows to the Lord in the presence of all his people.

Precious in the sight of the Lord is the death of his saints. O Lord, truly I am your servant; I am your servant, the son of your maidservant; you have freed me from my chains.

I will sacrifice a thank offering to you and call on the name of the Lord. I will fulfill my vows to the Lord in the presence of all his people, in the courts of the house of the Lord—in your midst, O Jerusalem.

Praise the Lord.

PSALM 117

The 117th psalm is a prophecy of Christ, that all the world should praise him and worship him in his kingdom. In this kingdom, nothing reigns but grace and truth, that is, the forgiveness of sins, eternal life, and all joy and comfort over sins, death, and all evil. This psalm is abundantly enough explained in our commentary.

[From Luther's commentary on Psalm 117:] I certainly believe that there is not one who truly knows everything the Holy Spirit says in this short psalm. If they were forced to teach or instruct someone from it, they would not know at which end to begin. To put these vicious people to shame and to honor God's Word, I have taken it upon myself to interpret this psalm, so that one may see how clear God's Word is, how simple, and yet how altogether . . . inexhaustible in power and virtue. It renews and refreshes the heart, restoring, relieving, comforting, and strengthening us constantly. (Luther's Works, American Edition 14:8)

PSALM 117

Praise the Lord, all you nations; extol him, all you peoples. For great is his love toward us, and the faithfulness of the Lord endures forever.
Praise the Lord.

PSALM 118

The 118th psalm is a psalm of thanks and my dearest, most beloved *Confitemini* [the Latin title of the psalm]. It gives thanks and also prophesies of the Christian and of Christ, the rejected cornerstone.

[From Luther's commentary on Psalm 118:] This psalm is a general statement of thanksgiving for all the kindnesses God daily and unceasingly showers on all men, both good and evil. . . . This psalm praises God especially for the greatest benefit he bestowed on the world, namely, for Christ and his kingdom of grace—first promised and now revealed. (Luther's Works, American Edition 14:47)

PSALM 118

Give thanks to the Lord, for he is good; his love endures forever.

Let Israel say: "His love endures forever." Let the house of Aaron say: "His love endures forever." Let those who fear the Lord say: "His love endures forever."

In my anguish I cried to the Lord, and he answered by setting me free. The Lord is with me; I will not be afraid. What can man do to me? The Lord is with me; he is my helper. I will look in triumph on my enemies.

It is better to take refuge in the Lord than to trust in man. It is better to take refuge in the Lord than to trust in princes.

All the nations surrounded me, but in the name of the Lord I cut them off. They surrounded me on every side, but in the name of the Lord I cut them off. They swarmed around me like bees, but they died out as quickly as burning thorns; in the name of the Lord I cut them off.

I was pushed back and about to fall, but the Lord helped me. The Lord is my strength and my song; he has become my salvation.

Shouts of joy and victory resound in the tents of the righteous: "The Lord's right hand has done mighty things! The Lord's right hand is lifted high; the Lord's right hand has done mighty things!"

I will not die but live, and will proclaim what the Lord has done. The Lord has chastened me severely, but he has not given me over to death.

Open for me the gates of righteousness; I will enter and give thanks to the Lord. This is the gate of the Lord through which the righteous may enter. I will give you thanks, for you answered me; you have become my salvation.

The stone the builders rejected has become the capstone; the Lord has done this, and it is marvelous in our eyes. This is the day the Lord has made; let us rejoice and be glad in it.

O Lord, save us; O Lord, grant us success. Blessed is he who comes in the name of the Lord. From the house of the Lord we bless you. The Lord is God, and he has made his light shine upon us. With boughs in hand, join in the festal procession up to the horns of the altar.

You are my God, and I will give you thanks; you are my God, and I will exalt you.

Give thanks to the Lord, for he is good; his love endures forever.

PSALM 119

The 119th psalm is a long psalm, containing prayers, comforts, instructions, and thanks in great number. It is chiefly written to make us excited about God's Word. It praises God's Word throughout and warns us against both the false teachers and against boredom and contempt for the Word. Therefore it is primarily to be counted among the psalms of comfort. Its primary concern is that we have God's Word in its purity and hear it gladly. From this concern, then, come powerful prayers, instructions, thanks, prophecies, worship of God, suffering, and all that pleases God and grieves the devil. But where one despises the Word and is satiated by it, there all these cease. For where the Word is not purely taught, there is truly an abundance of prayers, instructions, comforts, worship, suffering, and prophecies—but totally false and condemned! For it is then only service to the devil, who is thus impure with all his heretics.

PSALM 119:1–8

Blessed are they whose ways are blameless, who walk according to the law of the Lord. Blessed are they who keep his statutes and seek him with all their heart. They do nothing wrong; they walk in his ways. You have laid down precepts that are to be fully obeyed. Oh, that my ways were steadfast in obeying your decrees! Then I would not be put to shame when I consider all your commands. I will praise you with an upright heart as I learn your righteous laws. I will obey your decrees; do not utterly forsake me.

PSALM 119:9–16

How can a young man keep his way pure? By living according to your word. I seek you with all my heart; do not let me stray from your commands. I have hidden your word in my heart that I might not sin against you. Praise be to you, O Lord; teach me your decrees. With my lips I recount all the laws that come from your mouth. I rejoice in following your statutes as one rejoices in great riches. I meditate on your precepts and consider your ways. I delight in your decrees; I will not neglect your word.

PSALM 119:17–24

Do good to your servant, and I will live; I will obey your word. Open my eyes that I may see wonderful things in your law. I am a stranger on earth; do not hide your commands from me. My soul is consumed with longing for your laws at all times. You rebuke the arrogant, who are cursed and who stray from your commands. Remove from me scorn and contempt, for I keep your statutes. Though rulers sit together and slander me, your servant will meditate on your decrees. Your statutes are my delight; they are my counselors.

PSALM 119:25–32

I am laid low in the dust; preserve my life according to your word. I recounted my ways and you answered me; teach me your decrees.

Let me understand the teaching of your precepts; then I will meditate on your wonders. My soul is weary with sorrow; strengthen me according to your word. Keep me from deceitful ways; be gracious to me through your law. I have chosen the way of truth; I have set my heart on your laws. I hold fast to your statutes, O Lord; do not let me be put to shame. I run in the path of your commands, for you have set my heart free.

PSALM 119:33–40

Teach me, O Lord, to follow your decrees; then I will keep them to the end. Give me understanding, and I will keep your law and obey it with all my heart. Direct me in the path of your commands, for there I find delight. Turn my heart toward your statutes and not toward selfish gain. Turn my eyes away from worthless things; preserve my life according to your word. Fulfill your promise to your servant, so that you may be feared. Take away the disgrace I dread, for your laws are good. How I long for your precepts! Preserve my life in your righteousness.

PSALM 119:41–48

May your unfailing love come to me, O Lord, your salvation according to your promise; then I will answer the one who taunts me, for I trust in your word. Do not snatch the word of truth from my mouth, for I have put my hope in your laws. I will always obey your law, for ever and ever. I will walk about in freedom, for I have sought out your precepts. I will speak of your statutes before kings and will not be put to shame, for I delight in your commands because I love them. I lift up my hands to your commands, which I love, and I meditate on your decrees.

PSALM 119:49–56

Remember your word to your servant, for you have given me hope. My comfort in my suffering is this: Your promise preserves my life. The arrogant mock me without restraint, but I do not turn from your law. I remember your ancient laws, O Lord, and I find comfort in them. Indignation grips me because of the wicked, who have forsaken your law. Your decrees are the theme of my song wherever I lodge. In the night I remember your name, O Lord, and I will keep your law. This has been my practice: I obey your precepts.

PSALM 119:57–64

You are my portion, O Lord; I have promised to obey your words. I have sought your face with all my heart; be gracious to me according to your promise. I have considered my ways and have turned my steps to your statutes. I will hasten and not delay to obey your commands. Though the wicked bind me with ropes, I will not forget your law. At midnight I rise to give you thanks for your righteous laws. I am a friend to all who fear you, to all who follow your precepts. The earth is filled with your love, O Lord; teach me your decrees.

PSALM 119:65–72

Do good to your servant according to your word, O Lord. Teach me knowledge and good judgment, for I believe in your commands. Before I was afflicted I went astray, but now I obey your word. You are good, and what you do is good; teach me your decrees. Though the arrogant have smeared me with lies, I keep your precepts with all my heart. Their hearts are callous and unfeeling, but I delight in your law. It was good for me to be afflicted so that I might learn your decrees. The law from your mouth is more precious to me than thousands of pieces of silver and gold.

PSALM 119:73–80

Your hands made me and formed me; give me understanding to learn your commands. May those who fear you rejoice when they see me, for I have put my hope in your word. I know, O Lord, that your laws are righteous, and in faithfulness you have afflicted me. May your unfailing love be my comfort, according to your promise to your servant. Let your compassion come to me that I may live, for your law is my delight. May the arrogant be put to shame for wronging me without cause; but I will meditate on your precepts. May those who fear you turn to me, those who understand your statutes. May my heart be blameless toward your decrees, that I may not be put to shame.

PSALM 119:81–88

My soul faints with longing for your salvation, but I have put my hope in your word. My eyes fail, looking for your promise; I say, "When will you comfort me?" Though I am like a wineskin in the smoke, I do not forget your decrees. How long must your servant wait? When will you punish my persecutors? The arrogant dig pitfalls for me, contrary to your law. All your commands are trustworthy; help me, for men persecute me without cause. They almost wiped me from the earth, but I have not forsaken your precepts. Preserve my life according to your love, and I will obey the statutes of your mouth.

PSALM 119:89–96

Your word, O Lord, is eternal; it stands firm in the heavens. Your faithfulness continues through all generations; you established the earth, and it endures. Your laws endure to this day, for all things serve you. If your law had not been my delight, I would have perished in my affliction. I will never forget your precepts, for by them you have preserved my life. Save me, for I am yours; I have sought out your precepts. The wicked are waiting to destroy me, but I will ponder your statutes. To all perfection I see a limit; but your commands are boundless.

PSALM 119:97–104

Oh, how I love your law! I meditate on it all day long. Your commands make me wiser than my enemies, for they are ever with me. I have more insight than all my teachers, for I meditate on your statutes. I have more understanding than the elders, for I obey your precepts. I have kept my feet from every evil path so that I might obey your word. I have not departed from your laws, for you yourself have taught me. How sweet are your words to my taste, sweeter than honey to my mouth! I gain understanding from your precepts; therefore I hate every wrong path.

PSALM 119:105–112

Your word is a lamp to my feet and a light for my path. I have taken an oath and confirmed it, that I will follow your righteous laws. I have suffered much; preserve my life, O Lord, according to your word. Accept, O Lord, the willing praise of my mouth, and teach me your laws. Though I constantly take my life in my hands, I will not forget your law. The wicked have set a snare for me, but I have not strayed from your precepts. Your statutes are my heritage forever; they are the joy of my heart. My heart is set on keeping your decrees to the very end.

PSALM 119:113–120

I hate double-minded men, but I love your law. You are my refuge and my shield; I have put my hope in your word. Away from me, you evildoers, that I may keep the commands of my God! Sustain me according to your promise, and I will live; do not let my hopes be dashed. Uphold me, and I will be delivered; I will always have regard for your decrees. You reject all who stray from your decrees, for their deceitfulness is in vain. All the wicked of the earth you discard like dross; therefore I love your statutes. My flesh trembles in fear of you; I stand in awe of your laws.

PSALM 119:121–128

I have done what is righteous and just; do not leave me to my oppressors.Ensure your servant's well-being; let not the arrogant oppress me. My eyes fail, looking for your salvation, looking for your righteous promise. Deal with your servant according to your love and teach me your decrees. I am your servant; give me discernment that I may understand your statutes. It is time for you to act, O Lord; your law is being broken. Because I love your commands more than gold, more than pure gold, and because I consider all your precepts right, I hate every wrong path.

Psalm 119:129–136

Your statutes are wonderful; therefore I obey them. The unfolding of your words gives light; it gives understanding to the simple. I open my mouth and pant, longing for your commands. Turn to me and have mercy on me, as you always do to those who love your name. Direct my footsteps according to your word; let no sin rule over me. Redeem me from the oppression of men, that I may obey your precepts. Make your face shine upon your servant and teach me your decrees. Streams of tears flow from my eyes, for your law is not obeyed.

Psalm 119:137–144

Righteous are you, O Lord, and your laws are right. The statutes you have laid down are righteous; they are fully trustworthy. My zeal wears me out, for my enemies ignore your words. Your promises have been thoroughly tested, and your servant loves them. Though I am lowly and despised, I do not forget your precepts. Your righteousness is everlasting and your law is true. Trouble and distress have come upon me, but your commands are my delight. Your statutes are forever right; give me understanding that I may live.

Psalm 119:145–152

I call with all my heart; answer me, O Lord, and I will obey your decrees. I call out to you; save me and I will keep your statutes. I rise before dawn and cry for help; I have put my hope in your word. My eyes stay open through the watches of the night, that I may meditate on your promises. Hear my voice in accordance with your love; preserve my life, O Lord, according to your laws. Those who devise wicked schemes are near, but they are far from your law. Yet you are near, O Lord, and all your commands are true. Long ago I learned from your statutes that you established them to last forever.

PSALM 119:153–160

Look upon my suffering and deliver me, for I have not forgotten
your law. Defend my cause and redeem me; preserve my life according to your promise. Salvation is far from the wicked, for they
do not seek out your decrees. Your compassion is great, O Lord;
preserve my life according to your laws. Many are the foes who
persecute me, but I have not turned from your statutes. I look on
the faithless with loathing, for they do not obey your word. See how
I love your precepts; preserve my life, O Lord, according to your
love. All your words are true; all your righteous laws are eternal.

PSALM 119:161–168

Rulers persecute me without cause, but my heart trembles at your
word. I rejoice in your promise like one who finds great spoil. I
hate and abhor falsehood but I love your law. Seven times a day I
praise you for your righteous laws. Great peace have they who love
your law, and nothing can make them stumble. I wait for your
salvation, O Lord, and I follow your commands. I obey your statutes,
for I love them greatly. I obey your precepts and your statutes, for
all my ways are known to you.

PSALM 119:169–176

May my cry come before you, O Lord; give me understanding according to your word. May my supplication come before you; deliver
me according to your promise. May my lips overflow with praise,
for you teach me your decrees. May my tongue sing of your word,
for all your commands are righteous. May your hand be ready to
help me, for I have chosen your precepts. I long for your salvation,
O Lord, and your law is my delight. Let me live that I may praise
you, and may your laws sustain me. I have strayed like a lost sheep.
Seek your servant, for I have not forgotten your commands.

PSALM 120

The 120th psalm is a psalm of prayer. It laments and cries out against
the false teachers who commit murderous crimes, whose false teach-

ings penetrate like a sharp arrow, powerfully shot. They spread themselves out like fire in a juniper bush, which burns easily and well, for it is fat and thick and susceptible to fire. In the same way, the people are much, much more susceptible to false teachings (which harmonize well with reason) than to the true, as St. Paul (2 Tim. 4:3) also says about the itching ears.

PSALM 120

A song of ascents.

I call on the Lord in my distress, and he answers me. Save me, O Lord, from lying lips and from deceitful tongues.

What will he do to you, and what more besides, O deceitful tongue? He will punish you with a warrior's sharp arrows, with burning coals of the broom tree.

Woe to me that I dwell in Meshech, that I live among the tents of Kedar! Too long have I lived among those who hate peace. I am a man of peace; but when I speak, they are for war.

PSALM 121

The 121st psalm is a psalm of comfort in which the psalmist comforts us by his example, so that we may remain strong in faith and wait for God's help and protection. For although it appears as though he sleeps or slumbers so that we are struck down by the sun by day and the moon at night, yet it is not so, though we may think and feel it. For God watches and keeps us secure and does not let the sun strike us dead. This we will come to know for certain at last, though we can now only look forward to it.

PSALM 121

A song of ascents.

I lift up my eyes to the hills—where does my help come from? My help comes from the Lord, the Maker of heaven and earth.

He will not let your foot slip—he who watches over you will not slumber; indeed, he who watches over Israel will neither slumber nor sleep.

The Lord watches over you—the Lord is your shade at your right hand; the sun will not harm you by day, nor the moon by night.

The Lord will keep you from all harm—he will watch over your life; the Lord will watch over your coming and going both now and forevermore.

PSALM 122

The 122nd psalm is a psalm of thanks which gives thanks with joy for the Word of God, which in a specific city, namely Jerusalem, was given through a specific people, namely the Levites and kings, and received by specific hearers, namely the tribe of Israel. How much is it to be lamented that, seeking everywhere for God's Word and being nowhere able to find it, the children of Israel wound their way to idols. And we Christians did the same with our running to pilgrimages and winding our way to the cloister. But the holy church is our Jerusalem, and Christ is our temple, city, altar, and mercy seat, to which, from which, and with which we seek and hear his Word.

PSALM 122

A song of ascents. Of David.

I rejoiced with those who said to me, "Let us go to the house of the Lord." Our feet are standing in your gates, O Jerusalem.

Jerusalem is built like a city that is closely compacted together. That is where the tribes go up, the tribes of the Lord, to praise the name of the Lord according to the statute given to Israel. There the thrones for judgment stand, the thrones of the house of David.

Pray for the peace of Jerusalem: "May those who love you be secure. May there be peace within your walls and security within your citadels." For the sake of my brothers and friends, I will say, "Peace be within you." For the sake of the house of the Lord our God, I will seek your prosperity.

PSALM 123

The 123rd psalm is a psalm of prayer against the arrogant and the proud who despise and scorn God's Word and his little ones. Not only the nations considered the God and worship of the children of Israel to be a work of foolishness, yes, even error and sedition. Even among the Israelites themselves, the worshipers of idols and false gods, the false teachers with their multitudes, also arrogantly and securely despised and scorned the little land and the true teaching, as Psalm 12 and Psalm 14 above also lament.

So also today, our princes and rebellious spirits (who are "as holy as the Gospel itself") in an entirely princely and pious manner despise the poor preacher and the faithful worshiper of Christ and tread them underfoot—to say nothing of what our heathen, the spiritual lords, do, as well as their multitudes. We therefore are covered everywhere with contempt. But God is and will be gracious. Amen.

PSALM 123

A song of ascents.

I lift up my eyes to you, to you whose throne is in heaven. As the eyes of slaves look to the hand of their master, as the eyes of a maid look to the hand of her mistress, so our eyes look to the Lord our God, till he shows us his mercy.

Have mercy on us, O Lord, have mercy on us, for we have endured much contempt. We have endured much ridicule from the proud, much contempt from the arrogant.

PSALM 124

The 124th psalm is a psalm of thanks which thanks God that he protects his poor little band from the ruthless tyrants. He rescues them from the snares of the poisonous slanderer. These are as many and great as a great, deep water and flood against the little band. But though their teeth be ever so malevolent and angry, God is yet greater and knocks their teeth out and breaks the snares and rescues his own from them, as we still daily ourself experience.

PSALM 124

A song of ascents. Of David.

If the Lord had not been on our side—let Israel say—if the Lord had not been on our side when men attacked us, when their anger flared against us, they would have swallowed us alive; the flood would have engulfed us, the torrent would have swept over us, the raging waters would have swept us away.

Praise be to the Lord, who has not let us be torn by their teeth. We have escaped like a bird out of the fowler's snare; the snare has been broken, and we have escaped. Our help is in the name of the Lord, the Maker of heaven and earth.

PSALM 125

The 125th psalm is a psalm of thanks. It gives thanks that God will not forever tolerate the power of the ungodly teacher and officials over those who truly believe, teach, and hope in him. Therefore they need not be weary and for that reason fall away from the Word, but he would give all blessings to those who hope in him.

However, God will cut off and throw out the faithless with their crooked ways—the master as well as the student. We have seen and experienced this also in our own time among the rebellious spirits.

PSALM 125

A song of ascents.

Those who trust in the Lord are like Mount Zion, which cannot be shaken but endures forever. As the mountains surround Jerusalem, so the Lord surrounds his people both now and forevermore.

The scepter of the wicked will not remain over the land allotted to the righteous, for then the righteous might use their hands to do evil.

Do good, O Lord, to those who are good, to those who are upright in heart. But those who turn to crooked ways the Lord will banish with the evildoers.

Peace be upon Israel.

PSALM 126

The 126th psalm is a psalm of thanks for the deliverance from the captivity in Babylon. Whether it is made following that captivity or prior to it (as a prophecy for the comfort and hope for the coming deliverance, so that they may not despair) is of no concern. At the end the psalmist concludes that it happens—and always happens—to the saints that they suffer first before they can rejoice. Similarly, the world first rejoices before they get their suffering.

Therefore the saints sow with tears to reap afterward with joy. But (he says), such seed is excellent and precious seed to bring forth such a fruit. But before weeping, one cannot see that it is so precious and worthy before God. But God loves his saints so much that he regards even their death (which is truly the most abominable, accursed seed of the world) as more precious than all of the world's treasures and goods.

PSALM 126

A song of ascents.

When the Lord brought back the captives to Zion, we were like men who dreamed. Our mouths were filled with laughter, our tongues with songs of joy. Then it was said among the nations, "The Lord has done great things for them." The Lord has done great things for us, and we are filled with joy.

Restore our fortunes, O Lord, like streams in the Negev. Those who sow in tears will reap with songs of joy. He who goes out weeping, carrying seed to sow, will return with songs of joy, carrying sheaves with him.

PSALM 127

The 127th psalm is a psalm of instruction. It teaches us that worldly authority and household order are nothing less than God's gifts and rest only in his hand. For where he does not give peace and good government, there no wisdom, order, exertion, nor armor can hold onto peace. Where he does not give good fortune, with wife, children, and workers, there all care and work will be for nothing.

PSALM 127

A song of ascents. Of Solomon.

Unless the Lord builds the house, its builders labor in vain. Unless the Lord watches over the city, the watchmen stand guard in vain. In vain you rise early and stay up late, toiling for food to eat—for he grants sleep to those he loves.

Sons are a heritage from the Lord, children a reward from him. Like arrows in the hands of a warrior are sons born in one's youth. Blessed is the man whose quiver is full of them. They will not be put to shame when they contend with their enemies in the gate.

PSALM 128

The 128th psalm is a psalm of comfort in which the estate of marriage is splendidly praised. Marriage partners are given this great comfort: They should not look only at the trouble, work, discouragement, and discomfort they feel and experience in marriage, but rather the gracious will of God toward them, that their station and life are a gracious creation of God and are blessed by him. Therefore marriage is dear to him, and he gives it much more happiness and blessing than discomfort, if one only believes and adapts oneself to marriage and faithfully remains within it. Therefore in the beginning and middle of the psalm it says, "Those who fear the Lord . . . " When the godless go astray, on the other hand, it is no surprise.

PSALM 128

A song of ascents.

Blessed are all who fear the Lord, who walk in his ways. You will eat the fruit of your labor; blessings and prosperity will be yours. Your wife will be like a fruitful vine within your house; your sons will be like olive shoots around your table. Thus is the man blessed who fears the Lord.

May the Lord bless you from Zion all the days of your life; may you see the prosperity of Jerusalem, and may you live to see your children's children.

Peace be upon Israel.

PSALM 129

The 129th psalm is a psalm of thanks in which the people of Israel give thanks for the many deliverances that God has often done for them since the beginning. The books of Judges and of Kings show how often they were oppressed by the nations. They oppressed them severely for a long time and plowed long furrows on their back. They burdened them with yoke and fetters, until God raised up a deliverer for them to free them from their plows, yokes, and ropes. At the end the psalmist wishes for Israel (that is, prophesies of them) that all their enemies would be dried up and withered, which then was done. For all those peoples are gone; Israel alone remains. Thus all the heathen and enemies of Christ are like the grass on the roof that sprouts and grows as though it will produce much. But it withers before it is fully developed. It brings no fruit, and there is no blessing in it. So also the heathen, heretics, and other enemies when they rage and storm ultimately vanish, leaving neither seed nor mark behind them. The Christians however remain forever and ever.

PSALM 129

A song of ascents.

They have greatly oppressed me from my youth—let Israel say—they have greatly oppressed me from my youth, but they have not gained the victory over me. Plowmen have plowed my back and made their furrows long. But the Lord is righteous; he has cut me free from the cords of the wicked.

May all who hate Zion be turned back in shame. May they be like grass on the roofs, which withers before it can grow; with it the reaper cannot fill his hands, nor the one who gathers fill his arms. May those who pass by not say, "The blessing of the Lord be upon you; we bless you in the name of the Lord."

PSALM 130

The 130th psalm is a psalm of prayer which comes from the genuine davidic devotion and understanding. It confesses that before God no one is righteous, nor may he become righteous by his own work and righteousness, but rather, only through grace and forgiveness of sins, which God has promised. He relies on this promise and Word and comforts himself. He exhorts all of Israel that they should do the same and learn that with God is a throne of grace and redemption. Through him alone and no way else shall Israel be freed of sins, that is, "through forgiveness" (without which there is no grace) become righteous and blessed. Apart from this, he truly would be in the depths and would never stand before God.

Look! The true master and doctor of the Holy Scriptures is the one who understands what this means: the seed of the woman shall tread on the head of the serpent (Gen. 3:15), and through this seed all the nations of the world shall be blessed (Gen. 12:3). Therefore he places both a promise and a prophecy of Christ in this verse: "He will redeem Israel from all his sins." Upon this verse, and from it, comes the entire psalm.

A song of ascents.

Out of the depths I cry to you, O Lord; O Lord, hear my voice. Let your ears be attentive to my cry for mercy.

If you, O Lord, kept a record of sins, O Lord, who could stand? But with you there is forgiveness; therefore you are feared.

I wait for the Lord, my soul waits, and in his word I put my hope. My soul waits for the Lord more than watchmen wait for the morning, more than watchmen wait for the morning.

O Israel, put your hope in the Lord, for with the Lord is unfailing love and with him is full redemption. He himself will redeem Israel from all their sins.

PSALM 131

The 131st psalm is psalm of instruction. It speaks against the proud, stiff-necked saints who comfort themselves by placing confidence in their great services of worship and their great holiness, and not in the forgiveness of which the preceding psalm speaks. In contrast to the proud saints, the psalmist says, "I cannot travel so high and boast of my holiness as these people do, who rely on themselves. For whenever I have wanted to do so, not grounding and stilling my heart on God's grace (which is what it means to 'be still'), I become like a 'weaned child.' Without the nipple of the promise and grace, I cry day and night and have no peace in my conscience."

Therefore this is his conclusion: Let Israel and everyone trust and hope in God and depend only on his grace. Let no one take this nipple from you. I commend it to you, for the promised and coming Christ is in it.

[Note: Luther understood the verse about the weaned child not as a picture of a calm, contented child ("My soul is quiet like a child with its mother"), but rather as a picture of a child deprived of its mother's breast and therefore disturbed and upset ("If I do not quiet my soul, I am like an upset child in its mother's arms"). The only solution—in either picture—is to "nurse" on God's grace.]

PSALM 131

A song of ascents. Of David.

My heart is not proud, O Lord, my eyes are not haughty; I do not concern myself with great matters or things too wonderful for me. But I have stilled and quieted my soul; like a weaned child with its mother, like a weaned child is my soul within me.

O Israel, put your hope in the Lord both now and forevermore.

PSALM 132

The 132nd psalm is a psalm of prayer in which Solomon, or the people of Israel, pray for the preservation of the priesthood and the kingdom. That is, they pray for the spiritual and worldly authorities: for God's Word and temporal peace. For where these both stand well, things go well. He goes on to tell how such a prayer is not only heard, but that God has promised with an oath to preserve the kingdom and priesthood in Jerusalem and to dwell there himself. He will give all blessing and grace himself and bring their enemies down to disgrace, so long as they also keep his commandments and be obedient to him. Why however he calls the place of God's dwelling "Ephrathah" and the "fields of Jaar" is too long to comment on here and belongs in a commentary.

PSALM 132

A song of ascents.

O Lord, remember David and all the hardships he endured.

He swore an oath to the Lord and made a vow to the Mighty One of Jacob: "I will not enter my house or go to my bed—I will allow no sleep to my eyes, no slumber to my eyelids, till I find a place for the Lord, a dwelling for the Mighty One of Jacob.''

We heard it in Ephrathah, we came upon it in the fields of Jaar: ''Let us go to his dwelling place; let us worship at his footstool— arise, O Lord, and come to your resting place, you and the ark of your might. May your priests be clothed with righteousness; may your saints sing for joy.''

For the sake of David your servant, do not reject your anointed one.

The Lord swore an oath to David, a sure oath that he will not revoke: ''One of your own descendants I will place on your throne—if your sons keep my covenant and the statutes I teach them, then their sons will sit on your throne for ever and ever.''

For the Lord has chosen Zion, he has desired it for his dwelling: ''This is my resting place for ever and ever; here I will sit enthroned, for I have desired it—I will bless her with abundant provisions; her poor will I satisfy with food. I will clothe her priests with salvation, and her saints will ever sing for joy.

''Here I will make a horn grow for David and set up a lamp for my anointed one. I will clothe his enemies with shame, but the crown on his head will be resplendent.''

PSALM 133

The 133rd psalm is a psalm of instruction: That (in both the spiritual and worldly stations) we should live together harmoniously as friends, having one teacher, one authority, and that each should carry the burden of the other. He gives two comparisons: first, of the anointing oil which flows from Aaron's head over his beard and robes; second, of the dew which falls from Mt. Hermon onto Mt. Zion. Where things happen in this way, there God gladly dwells with all his grace, blessing, and life. But where disunity and faction prevail, there the devil dwells, and death, and all misfortune.

PSALM 133

A song of ascents. Of David.

How good and pleasant it is when brothers live together in unity! It is like precious oil poured on the head, running down on the beard, running down on Aaron's beard, down upon the collar of his robes. It is as if the dew of Hermon were falling on Mount Zion. For there the Lord bestows his blessing, even life forevermore.

PSALM 134

The 134th psalm is a psalm of instruction. It teaches and admonishes the priests and spiritual ones of their office. They should worship God faithfully and diligently, day and night praising God, preaching, and occupying themselves with his Word. As St. Paul also says to Timothy (2 Tim. 4:2 f.), they should continue faithful in their office. They should not concern themselves that people despise the Word and turn from it to fables. For where one discards God's Word, there both spiritual and worldly offices will fall as well—at the last, fall into error and, abandoned by God, fall into the devil's power.

However, where preaching continues, there he who made heaven and earth is always present to bless. For the sake of the Word, he helps and gives all blessings even to the unworthy and the unthankful. Let this psalm be sung by you pastors, preachers, bishops, and whoever sits in a spiritual office.

PSALM 134

A song of ascents.

Praise the Lord, all you servants of the Lord who minister by night in the house of the Lord. Lift up your hands in the sanctuary and praise the Lord.

May the Lord, the Maker of heaven and earth, bless you from Zion.

PSALM 135

The 135th psalm is a psalm of thanks. It calls the priests to give thanks, preach, and praise God for the wonders that he showed to the people in Egypt and Canaan, so that they never forget God and seek idols or other gods. This happens when one does not occupy oneself with—and diligently hold to—preaching and the praise of God, as it says in the next psalm. But when he judges his people, that is, preaches, teaches, and disciplines them, there he is certainly gracious to his servants. But where his Word is silenced and he does not judge or teach, there truly shall be great anger and no grace. Therefore think, you servants in the house of the Lord, and preach diligently of God and his works.

PSALM 135

Praise the Lord.

Praise the name of the Lord; praise him, you servants of the Lord, you who minister in the house of the Lord, in the courts of the house of our God.

Praise the Lord, for the Lord is good; sing praise to his name, for that is pleasant. For the Lord has chosen Jacob to be his own, Israel to be his treasured possession.

I know that the Lord is great, that our Lord is greater than all gods. The Lord does whatever pleases him, in the heavens and on the earth, in the seas and all their depths. He makes clouds rise from the ends of the earth; he sends lightning with the rain and brings out the wind from his storehouses.

He struck down the firstborn of Egypt, the firstborn of men and animals. He sent his signs and wonders into your midst, O Egypt, against Pharaoh and all his servants. He struck down many nations and killed mighty kings—Sihon king of the Amorites, Og king of Bashan and all the kings of Canaan—and he gave their land as an inheritance, an inheritance to his people Israel.

Your name, O Lord, endures forever, your renown, O Lord, through all generations. For the Lord will vindicate his people and have compassion on his servants.

174

The idols of the nations are silver and gold, made by the hands of men. They have mouths, but cannot speak, eyes, but they cannot see; they have ears, but cannot hear, nor is there breath in their mouths. Those who make them will be like them, and so will all who trust in them.

O house of Israel, praise the Lord; O house of Aaron, praise the Lord; O house of Levi, praise the Lord; you who fear him, praise the Lord. Praise be to the Lord from Zion, to him who dwells in Jerusalem.

Praise the Lord.

PSALM 136

The 136th psalm is a psalm of thanks and is perhaps the text to show priests how they should sing and preach. Namely, they should sing and preach of God and his wonderful deeds, that he is gracious and merciful and a true Savior. Therefore in each verse he repeats the line, "His love endures forever," with which the psalm is nearly overwhelmed. Truly nothing but grace, not human works or doctrines, should ever be preached. For human works and words have done no wonders such as these. They are not deserving of this worship, but rather only the grace and pure goodness of him who gives all. Gift! Gift, he says! Gift—free of charge! And Christ also stands hidden in the phrase. Such doctrine keeps in the people a pure faith and a right understanding of grace and the forgiveness of sins, against the rebellious and stiff-necked work-saints.

PSALM 136

Give thanks to the Lord, for he is good.
His love endures forever.
Give thanks to the God of gods.
His love endures forever.
Give thanks to the Lord of lords:
His love endures forever.

to him who alone does great wonders,
   His love endures forever.
who by his understanding made the heavens,
   His love endures forever.
who spread out the earth upon the waters,
   His love endures forever.
who made the great lights—
   His love endures forever.
the sun to govern the day,
   His love endures forever.
the moon and stars to govern the night;
   His love endures forever.
to him who struck down the firstborn of Egypt
   His love endures forever.
and brought Israel out from among them
   His love endures forever.
with a mighty hand and outstretched arm;
   His love endures forever.
to him who divided the Red Sea asunder
   His love endures forever.
and brought Israel through the midst of it,
   His love endures forever.
but swept Pharaoh and his army into the Red Sea;
   His love endures forever.
to him who led his people through the desert,
   His love endures forever.
who struck down great kings,
   His love endures forever.
and killed mighty kings—
   His love endures forever.
Sihon king of the Amorites
   His love endures forever.
and Og king of Bashan—
   His love endures forever.
and gave their land as an inheritance,
   His love endures forever.
an inheritance to his servant Israel;
   His love endures forever.

to the One who remembered us in our low estate
His love endures forever.
and freed us from our enemies,
His love endures forever.
and who gives food to every creature.
His love endures forever.
Give thanks to the God of heaven.
His love endures forever.

PSALM 137

The 137th psalm is a psalm of prayer in the person of captives in Babylon. It is a prayer for Jerusalem, that is, for God's Word and spiritual rule that lay completely destroyed; for thus it was assumed (with great reason) especially by those who fear God, as this psalm shows. Although Babylon and Edom greatly rejoiced at this destruction and mocked those who lamented it, yet they should not thereby escape, unrepentant and blameless, but rather shall be torn to pieces in return. Their children also shall be dashed on the rocks, and they shall have no descendants. This indeed happened to Babylon and shall also happen to our Edomites and Babylonians, who today rejoice, mocking both the poor church, torn to pieces, and the destruction of God's Word and worship. But for all that, Israel and God's Word shall remain forever and ever.

PSALM 137

By the rivers of Babylon we sat and wept when we remembered Zion. There on the poplars we hung our harps, for there our captors asked us for songs, our tormentors demanded songs of joy; they said, "Sing us one of the songs of Zion!"

How can we sing the songs of the Lord while in a foreign land? If I forget you, O Jerusalem, may my right hand forget its skill. May my tongue cling to the roof of my mouth if I do not remember you, if I do not consider Jerusalem my highest joy.

Remember, O Lord, what the Edomites did on the day Jerusalem fell. "Tear it down," they cried, "tear it down to its foundations!"

O Daughter of Babylon, doomed to destruction, happy is he who repays you for what you have done to us—he who seizes your infants and dashes them against the rocks.

PSALM 138

The 138th psalm is a general psalm of thanks for a variety of deliverances from the enemies. The psalmist wishes that Christ's kingdom would come and kings would receive his Word and doctrine and give thanks for it and worship him aright. They must learn that Christ's kingdom exists, that it sits on high, and that he helps the lowly who are stuck in woe and fear and comforts and rescues sinners and the miserable. He closes with the prayer that God would not abandon his kingdom and work thus begun but bring them to fulfillment in eternity.

PSALM 138

Of David.

I will praise you, O Lord, with all my heart; before the "gods" I will sing your praise. I will bow down toward your holy temple and will praise your name for your love and your faithfulness, for you have exalted above all things your name and your word. When I called, you answered me; you made me bold and stouthearted.

May all the kings of the earth praise you, O Lord, when they hear the words of your mouth. May they sing of the ways of the Lord, for the glory of the Lord is great.

Though the Lord is on high, he looks upon the lowly, but the proud he knows from afar. Though I walk in the midst of trouble, you preserve my life; you stretch out your hand against the anger of my foes, with your right hand you save me. The Lord will fulfill his purpose for me; your love, O Lord, endures forever—do not abandon the works of your hands.

PSALM 139

The 139th psalm is a psalm of thanks which praises God that he has provided for them so wonderfully and still reigns in all of his works, words, and thoughts. Whether the psalmist stands, walks, sleeps, or wakes—yes, even in his mother's womb, before he was made— God has been with him as he was being formed and will be with him as long as he lives.

It is as if he should say: Every human ability or power—how we live, what we do, speak, think, wherever and whenever, from where and to where we should go—it is all clearly but God's work and art. What then do the abominable ungodly do, who do not believe this but want to make themselves pious through their vexatious work? They want to have done what they do and then want to receive worship, honor, and glory from God on account of it. But they do not create so much as one word by themselves, indeed cannot create one thought by their own power. Moreover, they do not understand what they do, how they are created, how they live, speak, and think. Since then all that we are and do are God's work and power, how can they consider it to be their own noble work to make themselves godly, praise their free will, and deliver themselves from sin and death? Such people cannot rightly speak about God and his work. Protect us from this, O God, and bless my heart, so that I may remain in the true way that stands forever.

PSALM 139

For the director of music. Of David. A psalm.

O Lord, you have searched me and you know me. You know when I sit and when I rise; you perceive my thoughts from afar. You discern my going out and my lying down; you are familiar with all my ways. Before a word is on my tongue you know it completely, O Lord. You hem me in, behind and before; you have laid your hand upon me. Such knowledge is too wonderful for me, too lofty for me to attain.

Where can I go from your Spirit? Where can I flee from your presence? If I go up to the heavens, you are there; if I make my bed in the depths, you are there. If I rise on the wings of the dawn, if I settle on the far side of the sea, even there your hand will guide me, your right hand will hold me fast.

If I say, "Surely the darkness will hide me and the light become night around me," even the darkness will not be dark to you; the night will shine like the day, for darkness is as light to you.

For you created my inmost being; you knit me together in my mother's womb. I praise you because I am fearfully and wonderfully made; your works are wonderful, I know that full well. My frame was not hidden from you when I was made in the secret place. When I was woven together in the depths of the earth, your eyes saw my unformed body. All the days ordained for me were written in your book before one of them came to be.

How precious to me are your thoughts, O God! How vast is the sum of them! Were I to count them, they would outnumber the grains of sand. When I awake, I am still with you.

If only you would slay the wicked, O God! Away from me, you bloodthirsty men! They speak of you with evil intent; your adversaries misuse your name. Do I not hate those who hate you, O Lord, and abhor those who rise up against you? I have nothing but hatred for them; I count them my enemies.

Search me, O God, and know my heart; test me and know my anxious thoughts. See if there is any offensive way in me, and lead me in the way everlasting.

PSALM 140

The 140th psalm is a psalm of prayer against the proud, wicked saints who place many traps and annoyances in the right way, against God's Word. They threaten and rage against all those who do not praise and follow their errors. The psalm prays that their plans may not succeed but rather may fall on their own head and that it will happen to them as to Pharaoh in the Red Sea, that the storm may hurl them into the sea and they may be drowned. Thus may such evil mouths be silenced and the believers remain before God forever.

PSALM 140

For the director of music. A psalm of David.

Rescue me, O Lord, from evil men; protect me from men of violence, who devise evil plans in their hearts and stir up war every day. They make their tongues as sharp as a serpent's; the poison of vipers is on their lips.

Keep me, O Lord, from the hands of the wicked; protect me from men of violence who plan to trip my feet. Proud men have hidden a snare for me; they have spread out the cords of their net and have set traps for me along my path.

O Lord, I say to you, "You are my God." Hear, O Lord, my cry for mercy. O Sovereign Lord, my strong deliverer, who shields my head in the day of battle—do not grant the wicked their desires, O Lord; do not let their plans succeed, or they will become proud.

Let the heads of those who surround me be covered with the trouble their lips have caused. Let burning coals fall upon them; may they be thrown into the fire, into miry pits, never to rise. Let slanderers not be established in the land; may disaster hunt down men of violence.

I know that the Lord secures justice for the poor and upholds the cause of the needy. Surely the righteous will praise your name and the upright will live before you.

PSALM 141

The 141st psalm is a psalm of prayer. He prays that he may be preserved from the ungodly teachers, who appear to be friendly and speak with smooth word when threats do not work. It is better for me (he says) that righteous teachers rebuke me and condemn my righteousness, than that the godless praise me.

And if, in the meantime, evil comes upon me and I suffer cross and death and I am uprooted and torn apart, still it is better for me to trust in the Lord. Their hypocrisy will finally break their neck on a rock, that is, be suddenly overthrown and come to an evil end. Then they will see how bitter is their sweet teaching and how precious is my sour doctrine. Their own doctrine, in which they are caught as in a net, will bring them down, while I pass by in safety.

PSALM 141

A psalm of David.

O Lord, I call to you; come quickly to me. Hear my voice when I call to you. May my prayer be set before you like incense; may the lifting up of my hands be like the evening sacrifice.

Set a guard over my mouth, O Lord; keep watch over the door of my lips. Let not my heart be drawn to what is evil, to take part in wicked deeds with men who are evildoers; let me not eat of their delicacies.

Let a righteous man strike me—it is a kindness; let him rebuke me—it is oil on my head. My head will not refuse it.

Yet my prayer is ever against the deeds of evildoers; their rulers will be thrown down from the cliffs, and the wicked will learn that my words were well spoken. They will say, "As one plows and breaks up the earth, so our bones have been scattered at the mouth of the grave."

But my eyes are fixed on you, O Sovereign Lord; in you I take refuge—do not give me over to death. Keep me from the snares they have laid for me, from the traps set by evildoers. Let the wicked fall into their own nets, while I pass by in safety.

PSALM 142

The 142nd psalm is a psalm of prayer, as of one imprisoned under the false teachers who forcefully push them away from the true faith and life. For among the people of Israel it was a constant, commonplace occurrence that the true prophets were persecuted and condemned for the sake of the true worship and Word of God. All their histories show this, and Christ and St. Stephen also bear witness to it (Matt. 5:12; 23:34; Acts 7:52). Therefore it is no wonder that so many psalms are written against the false prophets and teachers, since it so commonly happened. It has happened in the church also since the beginning and always happens, so that one may well indeed pray to God that he would deliver us from false teachers and from error. The history of the time of Elijah, King Ahab, and Jezebel serves as an example for these psalms, that all prophets must hide themselves, crawl away. Also in the time of Arius all orthodox bishops had to flee into exile. For the devil will not tolerate God's Word and his servants.

PSALM 142

A maskil of David. When he was in the cave. A prayer.

I cry aloud to the Lord; I lift up my voice to the Lord for mercy. I pour out my complaint before him; before him I tell my trouble. When my spirit grows faint within me, it is you who know my way. In the path where I walk men have hidden a snare for me. Look to my right and see; no one is concerned for me. I have no refuge; no one cares for my life.

I cry to you, O Lord; I say, "You are my refuge, my portion in the land of the living." Listen to my cry, for I am in desperate need; rescue me from those who pursue me, for they are too strong for me. Set me free from my prison that I may praise your name.

Then the righteous will gather about me because of your goodness to me.

PSALM 143

The 143rd psalm is a psalm of prayer. The psalmist prays for grace and forgiveness of sins, in the terror of his conscience. He is nearly pressed to despair by the enemies of faith, that is, the promoters of the law. These especially plague the distressed and timid conscience and drive it into darkness, that is, into despair and death with heavy burdens and unbearable doctrine of works, which they do not so much as touch with one of their fingers, as Christ says (Matt. 23:1).

But here the psalm shows that grace provides deliverance, not the judgment before which no one alive can stand. Of this all the ancient histories and works of the Lord also give witness. For all of the holy patriarchs of old placed their hope on God's love and grace and not on the judgment. As St. Peter also says (Acts 15:10), "Neither we nor our fathers could bear such a yoke, but rather we hope to be saved through the grace of Christ, just as they were."

I consider their works and examples of old (he says here), and I am comforted, for they were comforted and delivered from sin purely by grace, just as I am. Even Abraham himself was called from out of idolatry (Joshua 24:2). No praise of human righteousness or holiness has any value here at all, no matter how much the false prophets worry us.

PSALM 143

A psalm of David.

O Lord, hear my prayer, listen to my cry for mercy; in your faithfulness and righteousness come to my relief. Do not bring your servant into judgment, for no one living is righteous before you.

The enemy pursues me, he crushes me to the ground; he makes me dwell in darkness like those long dead. So my spirit grows faint within me; my heart within me is dismayed.

I remember the day of long ago; I meditate on all your works and consider what your hands have done. I spread out my hands to you, my soul thirsts for you like a parched land.

Answer me quickly, O Lord; my spirit faints with longing. Do not hide your face from me or I will be like those who go down to the pit. Let the morning bring me word of your unfailing love, for I have put my trust in you.

Show me the way I should go, for to you I lift up my soul. Rescue me from my enemies, O Lord, for I hide myself in you. Teach me to do your will, for you are my God; may your good Spirit lead me on level ground.

For your name's sake, O Lord, preserve my life; in your righteousness, bring me out of trouble. In your unfailing love, silence my enemies; destroy all my foes, for I am your servant.

PSALM 144

The 144th psalm is a psalm of thanks for kings and those in authority. David, a king who has to wage war and rule, gives thanks to God with this psalm. He confesses that victory, good fortune, and success—whether in conflict or in government—are gifts of God and do not come from human power and ability. Little does human wisdom know how to keep subjects under authority and to rule land and people well. For how should he be capable of these great things when he is nothing and passes away like a shadow?

Instead, the Lord does this. He sends forth lightning—sending discouraged and frightened hearts to the army and humble hearts among the people. Where he thus touches the mountains and the multitudes, so that they are in fear before him, there it is good to fight and rule, for there victory and good fortune follow—as well as this fear. Yet how can one, being only flesh and blood, bring about this fear?

Then he prays against his own people and rebukes their foolishness. For the people of Israel, having the renown of being the people of God, were nevertheless proud, stiff-necked, disobedient, rebellious, covetous, jealous, and faithless, as indeed they showed by their opposition to Moses, David, and other kings. And although they saw that David fought and ruled with miraculous wonders, as did Moses, yet they were no better and did not inquire about God or faith in God.

"What God? What faith? As long as we have beautiful children, houses, cattle, many possessions, and enjoyable days, we are a blessed people. And, in addition, we have prophets enough, who teach us that God's people are those for whom things go well. Those for whom things go badly are not of God.'' Whereas in fact things go badly for all the saints—for the reason that they trust in God.

You have now rescued me, David says, from the murderous sword of Goliath. You have given me victory over other kings. Therefore preserve me also from this ungodly, evil, false people, who listen to neither God nor man. They are peasants and brutes, yes, truly swine, who are concerned for nothing but their own belly. It is harder and more dangerous to rule over them than to continually be at war.

He calls them foreign children, for they want to be the foremost children of God, and yet they are foreigners, strangers, and worse than heathen. They praise God with their mouths, while their heart is far from him.

PSALM 144

Of David.

Praise be to the Lord my Rock, who trains my hands for war, my fingers for battle. He is my loving God and my fortress, my stronghold and my deliverer, my shield, in whom I take refuge, who subdues peoples under me.

O Lord, what is man that you care for him, the son of man that you think of him? Man is like a breath; his days are like a fleeting shadow.

Part your heavens, O Lord, and come down; touch the mountains, so that they smoke. Send forth lightning and scatter the enemies; shoot your arrows and rout them. Reach down your hand from on high; deliver me and rescue me from the mighty waters, from the hands of foreigners whose mouths are full of lies, whose right hands are deceitful.

I will sing a new song to you, O God; on the ten-stringed lyre I will make music to you, to the One who gives victory to kings, who delivers his servant David from the deadly sword.

Deliver me and rescue me from the hands of foreigners whose mouths are full of lies, whose right hands are deceitful.

Then our sons in their youth will be like well-nurtured plants, and our daughters will be like pillars carved to adorn a palace. Our barns will be filled with every kind of provision. Our sheep will increase by thousands, by tens of thousands in our fields; our oxen will draw heavy loads. There will be no breaching of walls, no going into captivity, no cry of distress in our streets.

Blessed are the people of whom this is true; blessed are the people whose God is the Lord.

PSALM 145

The 145th psalm is a psalm of thanks for the kingdom of Christ, which was to come. It strongly urges the high, exalted work of praising God and glorifying his power and kingdom. For Christ's kingdom and power are hidden under the cross. If the cross were not extolled through preaching, teaching, and confession, who could have ever thought of it, to say nothing of knowing it? But such is his kingdom and power, that he aided the fallen, called the needy to himself, made sinners godly, and brought the dead to life. Yes, he is the one who gives food to all, who hears the call of his saints, does what they desire, protects them.

PSALM 145

A psalm of praise. Of David.

I will exalt you, my God the King; I will praise your name for ever and ever. Every day I will praise you and extol your name for ever and ever.

Great is the Lord and most worthy of praise; his greatness no one can fathom. One generation will commend your works to another; they will tell of your mighty acts. They will speak of the glorious splendor of your majesty, and I will meditate on your wonderful works. They will tell of the power of your awesome works, and I will proclaim your great deeds. They will celebrate your abundant goodness and joyfully sing of your righteousness.

The Lord is gracious and compassionate, slow to anger and rich in love. The Lord is good to all; he has compassion on all he has made. All you have made will praise you, O Lord; your saints will extol you. They will tell of the glory of your kingdom and speak of your might, so that all men may know of your mighty acts and the glorious splendor of your kingdom. Your kingdom is an everlasting kingdom, and your dominion endures through all generations.

The Lord is faithful to all his promises and loving toward all he has made. The Lord upholds all those who fall and lifts up all who are bowed down. The eyes of all look to you, and you give them their food at the proper time. You open your hand and satisfy the desires of every living thing.

The Lord is righteous in all his ways and loving toward all he has made. The Lord is near to all who call on him, to all who call on him in truth. He fulfills the desires of those who fear him; he hears their cry and saves them. The Lord watches over all who love him, but all the wicked he will destroy.

My mouth will speak in praise of the Lord. Let every creature praise his holy name for ever and ever.

PSALM 146

The 146th psalm is a psalm of thanks. It teaches at the same time that one should trust in God and not in princes, as the abominable world, flesh, and blood do. For God is the only one who can truly help in all kind of need, and he helps so that it can really be called being helped. Human help is so uncertain and does not last. For we ourselves do not know the length of our life.

PSALM 146

Praise the Lord.

Praise the Lord, O my soul. I will praise the Lord all my life; I will sing praise to my God as long as I live.

Do not put your trust in princes, in mortal men, who cannot save. When their spirit departs, they return to the ground; on that very day their plans come to nothing.

Blessed is he whose help is the God of Jacob, whose hope is in the Lord his God, the Maker of heaven and earth, the sea, and everything in them—the Lord, who remains faithful forever. He upholds the cause of the oppressed and gives food to the hungry. The Lord sets prisoners free, the Lord gives sight to the blind, the Lord lifts up those who are bowed down, the Lord loves the righteous. The Lord watches over the alien and sustains the fatherless and the widow, but he frustrates the ways of the wicked.

The Lord reigns forever, your God, O Zion, for all generations.

Praise the Lord.

PSALM 147

The 147th psalm is a psalm of thanks for various kindnesses and mighty works of God—first, toward Israel and Jerusalem, then to all who thirst. He gives rain and water to all creatures and does not let the least little bird go hungry, even the most useless raven. How much more then shall he care for us, especially those who trust in his goodness and not in human strength or horses? But above all, to Jerusalem, where his Word and his dwelling are, he gives peace, grain, and all they need. For Jerusalem and Israel have the advantage that they have God's Word and worship before all the nations; therefore he has done more miracles for them. He will also be much more recognized there in the daily wonders such as rain, snow, ice, than by the faithless who do not have God's Word or do not heed it. These people cannot see any work or wonder of God, though they enjoy them daily with their five senses, root in them, and devour them like swine. For they did not know God, because they do not hear or pay attention to his Word.

PSALM 147

Praise the Lord.

How good it is to sing praises to our God, how pleasant and fitting to praise him!

The Lord builds up Jerusalem; he gathers the exiles of Israel. He heals the brokenhearted and binds up their wounds.

He determines the number of the stars and calls them each by name. Great is our Lord and mighty in power; his understanding has no limit. The Lord sustains the humble but casts the wicked to the ground.

Sing to the Lord with thanksgiving; make music to our God on the harp. He covers the sky with clouds; he supplies the earth with rain and makes grass grow on the hills. He provides food for the cattle and for the young ravens when they call.

His pleasure is not in the strength of the horse, nor his delight in the legs of a man; the Lord delights in those who fear him, who put their hope in his unfailing love.

Extol the Lord, O Jerusalem; praise your God, O Zion, for he strengthens the bars of your gates and blesses your people within you. He grants peace to your borders and satisfies you with the finest of wheat.

He sends his command to the earth; his word runs swiftly. He spreads the snow like wool and scatters the frost like ashes. He hurls down his hail like pebbles. Who can withstand his icy blast? He sends his word and melts them; he stirs up his breezes, and the waters flow.

He has revealed his word to Jacob, his laws and decrees to Israel. He has done this for no other nation; they do not know his laws.

Praise the Lord.

PSALM 148

The 148th psalm is a psalm of thanks which excites and exhorts all creatures in heaven and earth to praise God—especially his saints, the children of Israel, who worship him, that is, have his Word and worship. And note that this psalm confirms all the stations of life— kings, judges, old, young. All are created by God and are good and honorable. For if the office of king or of judge were evil and not God-given, one could not in such an office praise God. But where there are kings and judges, there will also be subjects, servants, hangmen, soldiers, laborers, farmers, townspeople; where there are young and old, there will be married people, children, and household servants. All are honorable and good and show that their Creator is good. Rightfully, all of creation should be nothing but a tongue, always praising this great goodness of God. If you want to know how good a thing is, then take whatever you will and say: "If there were no fire . . .," or again, "If there were no sun . . ." "If there were no hangman . . ." "If there were no woman . . ." and so on. Then you will see why one should thank God.

PSALM 148

Praise the Lord.

Praise the Lord from the heavens, praise him in the heights above. Praise him, all his angels, praise him, all his heavenly hosts. Praise him, sun and moon, praise him, all you shining stars. Praise him, you highest heavens and you waters above the skies. Let them praise the name of the Lord, for he commanded and they were created. He set them in place for ever and ever; he gave a decree that will never pass away.

Praise the Lord from the earth, you great sea creatures and all ocean depths, lightning and hail, snow and clouds, stormy winds that do his bidding, you mountains and all hills, fruit trees and all cedars, wild animals and all cattle, small creatures and flying birds, kings of the earth and all nations, you princes and all rulers on earth, young men and maidens, old men and children.

Let them praise the name of the Lord, for his name alone is exalted; his splendor is above the earth and the heavens. He has raised up for his people a horn, the praise of all his saints, of Israel, the people close to his heart.

Praise the Lord.

PSALM 149

The 149th psalm is a psalm of thanks for the blessing that God is gracious and merciful to his people and that they know that they have a gracious God and that they rightly should rejoice. They have this blessing or grace—which is rightly called the forgiveness of sins—that God will not avenge how evil and sinful they are. Therefore this psalm in reality belongs in the New Testament. It calls itself a new song to sing to the King of Zion, whom they should praise on their couches, that is, in the church where they come together. (Similarly, Isaiah called the churches and altars, in which Israel committed fornication—that is, idolatry—couches or beds.)

Again, it belongs to the New Testament to have a sharp sword in hand to punish the heathen, to throw the kings in stocks and dungeons, and to take vengeance, as it is written. This is the vengeance that is spoken of in the Scriptures, that Abraham's seed should strike down idolatry in all the world through the Gospel, the spiritual sword, taking prisoner all the holiness of the kings and the wise and subject them to Christ, as Paul says in 2 Cor. 10:5.

PSALM 149

Praise the Lord.

Sing to the Lord a new song, his praise in the assembly of the saints.

Let Israel rejoice in their Maker; let the people of Zion be glad in their King. Let them praise his name with dancing and make music to him with tambourine and harp. For the Lord takes delight in his people; he crowns the humble with salvation. Let the saints rejoice in this honor and sing for joy on their beds.

May the praise of God be in their mouths and a double-edged sword in their hands, to inflict vengeance on the nations and punishment on the peoples, to bind their kings with fetters, their nobles with shackles of iron, to carry out the sentence written against them. This is the glory of all his saints.

Praise the Lord.

PSALM 150

The 150th psalm is a psalm of thanks written first of all for the people of Israel to praise God. For them his sanctuary—the firmament of his might, that is, his dwelling place, heaven, and castle—was in Jerusalem. Here also he showed his might with miracles and received the string music and the songs of the Jews, with which their praise and worship was accompanied. But for the Christian, preaching and the Gospel are our string music and worship.

Note that all psalms of thanks are nothing but promises for the poor, troubled conscience, saying as much as this: God is gracious and gladly forgives all sins and will give all comfort, so that we may find all blessings and comfort in him. Therefore this is openly a psalm of thanks and, at the same time, secretly a psalm of comfort—yes, even a psalm of instruction and a prophecy. All in one, it proclaims God's grace and teaches us to trust and believe in him. To this, may the same merciful God help us—our King and Lord, Jesus Christ, who with the Father and the Holy Spirit is praised forever. Amen.

PSALM 150

Praise the Lord.

Praise God in his sanctuary; praise him in his mighty heavens. Praise him for his acts of power; praise him for his surpassing greatness. Praise him with the sounding of the trumpet, praise him with the harp and lyre, praise him with tambourine and dancing, praise him with the strings and flute, praise him with the clash of cymbals, praise him with resounding cymbals.

Let everything that has breath praise the Lord.

Praise the Lord.